T0386545

THE

# J O U R N A L

OF

## FREDERICK HORNEMAN'S TRAVELS,

FROM

## CAIRO TO MOURZOUK,

THE

## CAPITAL OF THE KINGDOM OF FEZZAN,

## IN AFRICA.

IN THE YEARS 1797-8.

LONDON
DARF PUBLISHERS LIMITED
1985

First Published .. .. 1802
New Impression .. .. 1985

ISBN 1 85077 031 X

Reprinted by A. Wheaton & Co. Ltd, Exeter

# TABLE OF CONTENTS.

## APPENDIX.

---

### ERRATA.

Pag  6, Line  9, *for* roum, *read* rouin.
— 14,  —  7, *for* monachie, *read* menschie.
—  19,  — 10, *for* Logman, *read* Logmam.
—  —  — 13, *for* fennel, *read* flesh or meat.
—  —  — 14, *for* eyelid, *read* eyebrow.
— 46,  —  9, *after* watering-place, *insert* called *Ennaté.*
— 95,  —  6, *for* would, *read* wouldst.
—  —  — 27, *for* rare, *read* sure.
— 105,  —  9, *for* Ungila and Supah, *read* Augila and Siwah.
—  —  — 15, *after* is, *insert* not.
— 107,  — 17, *for* Burnû, *read* Burgû.
—  —  — 22, *for* SSW, *read* SSE.
— 112,  — 17, *for* the culture of their land, *read* their preparation of leather.

# INTRODUCTION.

The Society, instituted in the year 1788, for the purpose of exploring the Interior of Africa, in pursuing their *great* design, adopted *wise* and certain principles of procedure: they inquired, and then examined; they sought intelligence, and then directed research: their progress has been answerable to the just system of their pursuits and perseverance; and the Society, from the epoch of 1798, have been enabled to direct their efforts for further discovery, on data from actual visitation and experiment.

A volume of the transactions of the Society, printed in the years 1790—92, sets forth in detail, such communications respecting the Interior of Africa, as might be collected on inquiry from British Consuls; from the recital of Negro, or Moorish traders; or from that of Shereefs and others, who had passed with the caravans on religious pilgrimage, in different directions between Mecca and the various and remote stations of Mahomedans in Africa.

Those communications were, at the time, most inte-resting and useful; they afforded at once the incentive and the direction to farther inquiry; they opened new objects to commercial enterprize, and new matter for scientific speculation, on the productions of nature, and the manners and conditions of society, in a quar-ter of the globe hitherto unexplored: further, they pointed out the road, and facilitated the means, of as-certaining the truth of each account, and of estimating its importance and advantages by actual visitation and experiment.

Be it allowed, that the narrators spoke of what they had heard, as well as of what they had seen; let it be granted that they were mostly ignorant, credulous, or partially informed; and that, distinctively and in detail, the accuracy of their representations was little to be depended on; yet on points wherein their ac-counts agreed, they merited attention and regard; they *together* opened a general view of the society, and of the country; and afforded matter of such reasonable conjecture and inference, as might warrant and direct the course of further investigation. Reflecting on these and other relations made by unenlightened men, it ap-pears, that as the great continent of Africa, amidst its seas of sand, occasionally shews its Oasis, or fertile

isle, rising in each desert; so, in analogy to the face
of the country, does the blank and torpid mind of its
people, display occasionally notes of intelligence and
philanthropy; rich spots of genius, and partial scenes
of improved social establishment. Having passed whole
regions sterilized by apathy and ignorance, the result
of superstitions, prejudice, and oppression, the enlightened traveller comes to a sudden view of some rich
field of character, and contemplates with delight the
free-born spirit and sagacity of the Tuarick of Hagara,
and the ingenuity and benevolence of the Houssan.
To unfold and disseminate these germs of civilization,
is surely a noble task! What description of men and
country can be more interesting? whither could the
refinement of arts? whither could enlightened philo-
sophy better tend, to humanize and improve? whither
could the spirit of trade better direct its course? As
we speculate on the projected intercourse, the noblest
views open to the mind, anticipating reciprocal advantages: in the dispensation of intelligence and the arts
of peace, carrying therewith complacent manners to
rude and ferocious nations; and in a full compensation
to the enlightened adventurers, from new materials of
ingenuity and of commerce, and from new subjects
of scientific inference, extending the advancement of
human knowledge in all its branches.

The communications in question, operating on the minds of intelligent Members of the African Society, and giving a spur to the curiosity and enterprize of the agents they might employ, formed a suitable and necessary PREFACE to the undertaking and efforts for practical discovery, and for ensuring the advantages thence to be derived.

The compilation of various informations respecting Africa, had thus an intrinsic value, as affording premises of inquiry, and as giving encouragement and direction to adventure.

But further, and even immediately, wisdom and sagacity will extract truth from accounts, however contradictory, and useful and certain inference, from documents the most ambiguous or incomplete.

Efforts of rude ingenuity often suggest not only improvement but discovery; the rustic forms a lever to raise the mass, and the sagacity of the mechanic applies it to ascertain the weight.

Science often works with effect on the loose and disjointed materials which ignorance has heaped together; compares, arranges, and connects their

substances and forms; shews in their matter, construction, or decomposition, new uses ; derives new informations, and adds to the stock of human inventions
and knowledge.

Were it necessary to illustrate such position by
example, the writer would refer, as a special instance,
to the elucidations of Major Rennell on the communications in question : to that most accurate and acute
philosopher and geographer, the details have afforded
matter of enquiry and deduction of the highest import
to science.  By analysis, and a comparative view of
accounts given of journies and places, in reference to
the plans of D'Anville, and other geographers ; to
modern travels ; to ancient expeditions ; to descriptions of ancient writers ;  and above all, to those of the
father of history, Herodotus ; Major Rennell hath corrected the map of Africa, with a learning and sagacity
which *hath converted conjecture into knowledge;* and on
experience of those who have explored parts of that
great continent, given confidence to each future traveller who may visit its remotest regions.

Had the proceedings of the Society stopped here,
and its work been confined to the compilation above
alluded to, and to the comments of Major Rennell, the

usefulness of its institution would have been acknowledged by posterity.

But happily the Journal of Mr. Park's travels to the
Niger, and that of Mr. Horneman's journey from Cairo
to Mourzouk, will fully shew, that the attainments of
the Society are no longer narrowed to the mere rudiments of discovery, which tradition and ingenious
inference, alone before supplied.

Even under the inauspicious circumstances of wars
and revolutions which from nearly the date of the
establishment of the Society, have spread desolation
far and wide, and in the year 1798, reached to the
very capital of Africa; their chosen emissaries have
surmounted all the dangers and difficulties, which
these events superadded to the ordinary risk of enterprise.

It should not be omitted, that the traveller, (whose
work is now submitted to the public,) was further
indebted to the liberal and enlightened spirit, which
directs the genius of truly great men to foster useful
arts and sciences amidst the horrors of war; and give
orders to the armies under their command, to forbear
all molestation of the emissary from even an hostile

country, whose intentions and pursuits are directed to objects of common value and concern, to the nations of the world at large.

Under such patronage and protection from the General Bonaparte, and with his special passport and safeguard, Frederick Horneman safely reached the caravan passing from Mecca, and pursued, and accomplished his journey from Cairo to the kingdom of Fezzan ; which from the general resort of caravans to its capital, Mourzouk, may be considered as the proper post of direction and outfit, for his further travels to the remotest regions of Africa.

In planning the routes of Park and of Horneman, the Society availed itself of former communications, sagaciously discriminated the proper path of research, and have to exult in the success of each adventure. These emissaries have explored roads which shortly mercantile adventure will, and must enter. In this new race of commerce, shame indeed would it be to our national councils, could it possibly be supposed that from the default of patronage and support of Government, our commercial people may lose the start for a priority of factories and establishments of trade, and permit other nations to usurp the vantage ground which British enterprise, under the auspices of a patriotic and enlightened, but private institution, shall have explored, marked out, and prepared for them,

By Mr. Park's discoveries, a gate is opened to every commercial nation to enter and trade from the west to the eastern extremity of Africa. The navigable parts of the rivers Gambia and Niger are not so far distant, but that great facilities of trade may thence be derived, aided by the establishment of intermediate stations and points of intercourse. A considerable traffic is carried on by the natives for ostrich feathers, drugs, ivory, and gold, even without such advantage. On due direction and exertions of British credit and enterprise, it is difficult to imagine the possible extent to which the demand for our country's manufactures might arrive, from such vast and populous countries in the bosom of which *gold*, the great medium of commerce, is readily found ; and which would be sought for and brought into circulation with new avidity and success, in proportion as objects for the exchange, became known, desirable, and necessary to the people.

This subject has already been recommended by the Society, to the attention of Government ; and on the return of peace, it is not doubted, but it will be treated with a consideration and regard, suitable to the important interests which it involves.

When the thorny track of a Park or a Horneman is become the beaten road of the merchant, advantages of another sort will quickly follow; and the intercourse extend to the instruction of the naturalist and philosopher, to the promotion of civilization, and to the increase of the general stock of human knowledge and happiness.

Contemplating such accomplishment of the wise and benevolent purposes of their Institution, the patriotic members of this Society cannot but look back with exultation to the hour of its establishment, and they will with satisfaction recapitulate its means and progress, towards such happy termination of their labours.

Of those who transmitted accounts which they had received, concerning the people and country of Africa, Mr. Ledyard and Mr. Lucas were specially employed, with the further intent of progress into the heart of the country; for the purpose of ascertaining the truth of these recitals, the correcting them on personal information, and the elucidating, on actual survey, any

future plan for turning the knowledge thence derived
to account.

Mr. Ledyard died at Cairo, ere his eager and enterprising spirit could even start towards its object: Mr.
Lucas, deterred by impending difficulties and dangers,
proceeded not further than to Mesurata, seven days
journey S. E. of Tripoly; there collected informations
from the Shereef Imhammed, and traders of Fezzan,
and then measured his road back to Tripoly; and
shortly after returned to England.

The Society, with that persevering spirit which
ever distinguishes manly minds, engaged on sound
principles, and for noble purposes, were not appalled
by the death of one emissary, or the failure of another.

They sought out and appointed a new traveller, and
to take a new road. Mr. Ledyard was to have penetrated
from the east, Mr. Lucas from the north; Major Houghton
was appointed in the year 1790, to sail for the mouth
of the Gambia, and to traverse the country from west
to east: Major Houghton arrived on the coast of Africa
November 10, of that year, immediately commenced
his journey, ascended the Gambia to Medina, 900
miles (by the water-course) distant from the mouth of

the river, and thence proceeded to Bambouk and to the adjoining kingdom of Kasson; where, in September 1791, he unfortunately terminated his travels with his life, near to the town of Jarra. Mr. Park, who was engaged in the service of the Society, in 1795, more successfully followed the route of Major Houghton, and further explored to the banks of the Niger, to Sego, and to Silla, the first of that great line of populous and commercial cities, dividing the southern from the northern deserts of Africa; and the very existence of which, for centuries past, hath been rather matter of rumour than of information; and been made the subject of philosophic romance,* in default of authentic account and description.

The informations of Mr. Park were communicated to the Society at their annual Meeting in May 1798.

The year 1798 will ever be noted. as the memorable epoch, when the researches of this Society announced to the world the course of the Niger, from west to east; and, after the distance of 2300 years, corroborated the testimony of the Nasamones, and accounts of Herodotus, contested during that long period by ancient and later writers, and ultimately rejected

---

\* By Bishop Berkeley.

within the century past, by the learned D'Anville. But further, the settlements on its fertile shores, are by the informations of Park, derived from inquiries so near to the source, as now greatly to be depended on ; at least so far, as to give assurance of objects of commerce and learned inquiry, that will amply repay further research. The just motto of the Society is, " *quod non peractum, pro non inchoato est;*" its exertions and perseverance answer to it, and it is to be congratulated that the task is now easy, its accomplishment assured.

The writer of this Essay, not presuming to graft addition or observation on the intelligent and authentic Journal of Mungo Park, ventures a single comment, of import to the Society, and in justice to its agent.

Mr. Park has not only designated the route of *country* but of *men.* He hath marked the districts of population covering the great belt of land intersecting Africa from west to east, and at the same time hath noted the distinctions of Moor and Negro, in manners, prejudices, and government. He hath thereby given to the Society information of the *viaticum* of character and accomplishments proper and necessary to ensure the success of *their future agents :* he hath pointed out the roads to districts and cities of the greatest interest, and at the same time hath shewn the means of securing entrance and hospitable reception.

The Society hath availed itself of the intelligence; and a new emissary, Mr. Horneman, hath given his lesson full effect in an expedition which is the subject of the present Volume.

Of the further progress of this accomplished traveller, the Editor forbears to intimate design or suggestion.

The season of mere expectation and conjecture is gone by. It were idle indeed at this period of actual discovery, to hazard surmise for future correction on experiment.

At outset of the Society instituted for the purpose of exploring the Interior of Africa, it might have been proper to set forth, in glowing colours, all that was rumoured, and all that might be expected; well were general reports and ingenious inferences suited to rouze curiosity, to excite adventurous spirit, and to give a spring to the first movements and purposes of the Institution.

Such incentives are no longer necessary; and knowledge actually acquired demands, in the future display, merely accuracy and precision, as the guides to
further success.

The Society is confirmed in its purpose, and assured
of its objects and of the means of attainment.

Its travellers will not in future rush on with zealous
but unadvised curiosity; or hesitate as in the dark, and
on unfounded apprehensions; but, disciplined and
educated, proceed with a spirit corrected and confirmed by knowledge and precaution, towards certain
purposes and ends.

An adventurer may yet fail; but it is presumed the
adventure cannot, unless from failure of the funds and
resources of the Society; which, in this great and
opulent country, it would be a calumny on the gene-
rosity and patriotism of its people, for one moment to
anticipate as possible.

Yet let it be remembered, that the extent of our un-
dertakings can only be commensurate with our means.

Expense and charge attend our present inquiries;

and even a more advantageous extension of our researches apart, demands of much beyond what our
actual numbers and contributions can furnish, will be
necessary to ensure the effect of national advantage,
and turn to public account the successful experiment
of an enlightened and patriotic, but not numerous,
Association.

The Society cannot condescend to solicitation ; nor
is it necessary : it will suffice, that, emboldened by
success, they suggest to their countrymen, that, under
proper patronage, and with the means of extending
their researches, *the conclusion will be of advantage, to
Great Britain—to Africa—and to the World.*

### W. YOUNG,

SECRETARY TO THE AFRICAN SOCIETY.

# PREFACE TO THE JOURNAL, &c.

GIVING SOME ACCOUNT OF MR. FREDERICK HORNEMAN; OF THE PREPARATIONS FOR HIS VOYAGE; AND OF EVENTS PREVIOUS TO HIS LEAVING CAIRO.

At the time that Mr. Mungo Park, engaged in the service of the Society instituted for the purpose of exploring the Interior of Africa, was prosecuting discoveries eastward from the river Gambia, it was thought proper to extend their researches in another line of direction, and engage an emissary to explore that great continent, proceeding westward from the city of Cairo.

Early in the year 1796, Mr. F. Horneman offered himself to the Committee of the Society for this service; he appeared to be young, robust, and, in point of constitution and health, suited to a struggle with different climates and fatigues: in his manner and conversations he displayed temper, acuteness, and prudence: he was well apprized of the dangers and difficulties of the enterprize he was to engage in, and shewed a spirit and zeal for the undertaking, which strongly recommended him as a proper person to be employed for the carrying it into effect.

The Committee accordingly engaged his services; and observing in him such foundation of good ordinary education, as further attainments might readily be engrafted upon, they sent him, at the expense of the Society, to Gottingen ; there to study the rudiments and writing of the Arabic language, and, generally, such sciences as (in the result of due application of the knowledge acquired), might render any account of his future travels more interesting and useful to his employers, and to the public.

F. Horneman pursued the requisite studies for several months with great assiduity, under the tuition of Professors Blumenbach, Heeren, Hoffman, Tyschen, and Heyne; and in May, 1797, returned to England, properly instructed for his intended voyage. He was then introduced to a general meeting of the Society, when his engagement was approved of, and he was directed to proceed to Egypt with all convenient dispatch.

Passports from Paris were applied for, and granted, permitting him to pass through France; and in July, 1797, he left London on his way to Paris.

He was furnished with letters of introduction to several persons of literary distinction in that capital; and, on arrival, his reception was liberal and friendly, and proportionate to the lively interest which was every where taken in his scheme of enterprize, and in the means of promoting its success. He was invited to a meeting of the National Institute. The first members of that learned society tendered their patronage, encouragement, and assistance: Mr. Lalande furnished him with copies of his " Memoire sur L'Afrique."

Mr. Broussonet recommended him to Mr. Laroche, appointed Consul for Mogadore; and by this latter gentleman's means he made a further and most useful acquaintance with a Turk of distinction (a native of Tripoly), then resident at Paris. This Mussulman entered into the motives and plan of his travels with a liberal approbation, and a zealous interest in the success; which was little to have been expected from one of such persuasion and character. He gave Mr. Horneman letters of introduction, strongly recommending him to the friendship and protection of several leading Mahommedan merchants at Cairo, who were in the habits of trade with people of the remotest regions of Africa; and he added his own advice, and instructions for the journey.

Thus provided, Mr. Horneman, in August, left Paris for Marseilles, where he embarked the end of the month, and arrived at Alexandria the middle of September: he staid at Alexandria but a few days, and then went to Cairo, where he purposed residing some time, to study the language and manners of the Mograbins, or western Arabs, with whom he was to associate in his future travels. His own letter will best describe his further progress.

(TRANSLATION.)

" SIR,                                                    *Cairo, August* 31, 1798.

" In my last letter I mentioned my intentions of leaving Cairo about the end of May. The plague beginning to rage in the month of April, it became a proper and necessary precaution not only to defer my journey, but absolutely to shut myself up in my house.

My zeal for the undertaking I have engaged in, would have led me to break through this confinement and leave the city, with a view to join the merchants at their place of rendezvous, whence they were directly to depart for Fezzan, had not obstacles arising from the difficulty of procuring the necessary credits for my equipment prevented my immediate procedure.

" As soon as from abatement of the pestilence, I could safely go abroad, I met and renewed my acquaintance with several of the caravan, who remained in the city, expecting the return of others from Mecca. A French commercial house, on whom I had no letters of credit or other claim to confidence, than what arose from private friendship and esteem, having handsomely offered such advance of monies as I might require, I was enabled to prepare for my journey, and set out with this caravan, as soon as complete and ready for departure. All these designs were suddenly frustrated by the arrival of the French on the coast of Egypt. Those who formed the caravan at Cairo quickly dispersed; that from Mecca coming to join it was not yet arrived: myself and other Europeans were seized and confined in the castle, rather as a place of refuge from the indignation and fanaticism of the populace, than as a prison, and we remained there until the arrival of the French at Cairo.

" Soon after their coming, I made acquaintance with two of their learned men, Berthollet and Monge, they liberated and presented me to the Commander in Chief, and he received me with every mark of attention and goodness. His regard for science, and esteem of

learned men are too well known to render it necessary for me to
expatiate on these high qualities.  He promised me protection, he
offered me money or whatever was requisite to my undertaking,
and he directed the necessary passports to be prepared for me.

" I lost no time in seeking out my friends, the merchants of
Fezzan, and renewing my connections with them.  Gradually as the
public tranquillity became assured, they returned, one by one into
the city, till the whole were again assembled ; and fifteen days
have now passed, since we have been making preparations for our
final departure, actually fixed for the day after to-morrow.

" Commonly those who engage in an extraordinary enterprise,
consider means yet more extraordinary, as requisite to the success
of the undertaking : my opinion, and therewith procedure will be
founded on directly the contrary proposition.  The plan which I
have chalked out for my journey will be simple and easy to pursue.
You shall have it in a single line, " it is to travel as a Mahommedan
merchant of the caravan."  I am assured that under such character,
I can travel with the same surety as the natives of the country.

" Many of the caravan having been at Mecca, are aware that there
are numbers of good Mussulmen from various countries who speak
not Arabic, and who have different usages and customs ; and thus
simply attaining a knowledge of certain religious ceremonies
and prayers, there is no difficulty in passing generally as a
Mahommedan ; for as to a certain less equivocal criterion of a

personal nature, the delicacy of Mahommedan manners precludes any danger of inquiry.

" To travel as a Christian, will perhaps be impracticable for at least five years to come, for it is incredible how deep and strong an impression the expedition of the French has made on the minds of the pilgrims to and from Mecca: dispersed to their several homes they will carry an aggravated prejudice against Christians far and wide, and to the very heart of Africa.

" Should it be objected to me, that I risk a similar fate with that of Major Houghton, by travelling as a trader, my answer is, " that by travelling as a Mahommedan trader, I shall never travel alone; and with those too of the caravan, considered as one of the least of its merchants.

" In respect to my astronomical instruments, I shall take special care never to be discovered in the act of observation; should those instruments, however, attract notice, the answer is ready, " they are articles for sale;" nor is there fear that I should be deprived of them, whilst master of my price. My comrades know the value of gold at least better than myself. In a word, the merchants of our Fezzan caravan, are men of wealth, integrity, and enterprise; but Mahommedans, the most prejudiced and fanatic.

" I have not yet fixed or methodized my design, as to further journey into the interior of Africa; but I have made acquaintance with a man who has been at Bornou and Cashna, a place, from every account which I can collect, and particularly from the Jalabs, deserving my immediate attention after arrival at Fezzan.

" I expect to be at Fezzan by the beginning of November, and I should propose in the next year, setting out for the Agades and Cashna, residing in and exploring those countries during ten months, and then returning *via* Mecca or Senegambia. Should any necessity of the case oblige me to return to Tripoly, I should not consider my tour as complete, but (with permission of the Society,) hold myself in readiness for a further undertaking.

" I will write again from Fezzan, if I can do so without danger; the safest plan that occurs, is to pack up some bale of goods with an ordinary letter of advice in Arabic, making my real dispatch the package or covering of some article of trade.

" Pray write to and direct the English Consul at Tripoly, or elsewhere, never to make inquiry after me of the traders from Fezzan, and particularly when conveying any thing from me consigned to you. These people are of a very jealous and inquisitive temper, and any inquiries made after me by a Christian, might raise a thousand suspicions, and prove even of fatal consequence to me.

" Nay, should yourselves not hear of me these three years, make no inquiry. Under such precaution, my danger will not be that I travel as a trader and Mahommedan, but such only as results from climate and ordinary perils of voyage in these countries; which I trust successfully to oppose, with a good constitution and strength of body, and with courage and suitable temper of mind.

" It remains only for me to recommend to the Committee, the man whom I mentioned in a former letter. I met with the person in question, Joseph Frendenburgh, who was born in Germany, just on the eve of his intended departure from Cairo for his native country. I engaged and employed him as interpreter; and, pleased with the office, he offered to continue in my service, and attend me in my expedition. He had been ten or twelve years past forced to embrace the Mohammedan religion; had three times made the voyage to Mecca, and spoke perfectly both the Arabic and Turkish languages; in short, he was precisely the man that suited me. The connection with him will ensure me character and confidence from others, and indeed, without him, I should scarcely be able to pursue my journey, without actually embracing and professing Mahommedanism myself, I now well know him on ten months experience, and in just reliance on him, have no apprehension of the calamity incident to travellers, of being robbed by their servants.

" I shall consign to him the care of my camels and my horses, (for we merchants of the caravan all go armed, and on horseback,) he will further have the care of my merchandize, and altogether, I shall have leisure for my inquiries, and for attending to the general objects of my undertaking. The demands of this man are far from exorbitant, and I request of the Society, the attending to a just remuneration of his services, and specially, if in case of my death, he should faithfully preserve my journals and papers, and proceed with them to England.

" I have been in some doubt as to the means of sending this letter, but on my request, General Bonaparte has with great goodness, himself condescended to take charge of its safe conveyance.

" I hope my next will be from Fezzan, and that after three years, I shall be enabled to give account of the interior of Africa.

" I am, &c. &c. &c.

" FREDERICK HORNEMAN."

*To Mr. Edwards, Secretary to the Society,*
*instituted for exploring the interior of Africa.*

The above letter was transmitted to the African Committee, under the seal of General Bonaparte, who in addition to other marks of favour and protection shewn to the enterprise of Horneman, took on himself the care of forwarding his dispatches, as above stated.

Mr. Horneman's Journal of his Travels from Cairo to Fezzan commences five days after the date of this letter. It was by him written in German, and in that language transmitted to the Committee of the African Society. Under their direction, a translation of it was made by a native of Germany, sufficiently versed in the

English language, to render the sense of the original with truth and perspicuity; and, on collating his version, it appears to have been executed with fidelity and care. Some correction of foreign idioms and style was yet required : the Secretary, in performing this duty of Editor, has been attentive to the preserving not only the genuine descriptions, remarks, and precise meaning of the traveller, but likewise the spirit, and (at the same time) simplicity of narrative which characterizes his Journal; and, it is presumed, that on reference to the original, the translation offered in its present form will *yet* appear to be as nearly literal, as the different idioms and context of the English and German languages will admit of.

To the Journal now printed is added an Appendix, containing,

1st. A Note, on Mr. Horneman's Description of the Country and Antiquities of Siwah; with Reference to ancient Accounts of the Oasis and Temple of Ammon; by the Secretary, Sir William Young, Bart. F. R. S.

2d. A Memoir, containing various informations respecting the interior of Africa, transmitted from Mourzouk, in 1799, by F. Horneman.

3d. Geographical Elucidations of the Travels and of the Informations of F. Horneman, with Maps, by Major James Rennell, F. R. S.

4th. Remarks on the Language of Siwah, in a Letter to the Right Hon. Sir Joseph Banks, P. R. S. by William Marsden, Esq. F. R. S.

# TRAVELS

IN THE

# INTERIOR OF AFRICA.

## CHAPTER I.

### VOYAGE FROM CAIRO TO AUGILA.

### SECTION I.

*To Ummesogeir.*

THE merchants of Augila had appointed their rendezvous to be held at *Kardaffi*, a village in the vicinity of Cairo; where I joined them on September the 5th, 1798, and leaving that place the same day, in about an hour we reached the great body of the caravan, which yearly returns from Mecca through Cairo and Fezzan, to the western countries of Africa. The caravan was waiting for us at a small village called *Baruasch*: we halted at some little distance from the pilgrims, and encamped until the next morning; when the monotonous kettle-drum of our Sheik awakened us before rise of the sun, with summons to proceed on our journey.

I had not under-rated the difficulties of the journey; I was aware that many must arise, especially affecting myself, never having before travelled with a caravan, and being little acquainted with the customs and manners of those who composed it.  We had travelled from day-break till noon, and no indication appeared of halt or refreshment, when I observed the principal and richest merchants gnawing a dry biscuit and some onions, as they went on ; and was then, for the first time, informed, that it was not customary to unload the camels for regular repast, or to stop during the day-time, but in cases of urgent necessity.  This my first inconvenience, was soon remedied by the hospitality of some Arabs who were riding near me, and who invited me to partake of their provisions.

Soon after sun-set, our Sheik gave the signal for halting; and we pitched our tents.

My dragoman, or interpreter, might, even in Europe, have passed for a good cook ; and from remains of the provision which our hospitable friends at Cairo had supplied, was preparing an excellent supper, when an old Arab of Augila, observing his preparations, and that myself was unemployed, addressed me nearly as follows : " Thou art young, and yet dost not assist in preparing the meal of which thou art to partake : such, perhaps, may be a custom in the land of infidels, but is not so with us, and especially on a journey : thanks to God, we are not, in this desert, dependent on others, as are those poor pilgrims, but eat and drink what we ourselves provide, and as we please.  Thou oughtest to learn every thing that the meanest Arab performs, that thou mayest be enabled to asssit others in cases of necessity; otherwise, thou wilt be less esteemed, as being of less value than a  mere woman ; and many will think they may justly deprive thee of every thing in thy possession, as being un-worthy to possess any thing : (adding sarcastically,) perhaps thou art carrying a large sum of money, and payest those men well."

This remonstrance was not thrown away. I immediately assisted in every thing that was not beyond my force; and proportionally gained on the good opinion and esteem of my fellow-travellers, and was no longer considered as a weak and useless idler in their troop.

The next morning we set out early, and after a march of four hours, arrived at *Wadey-el-Latron*. The signal had been made to halt, for the purpose of collecting fresh water, when a troop of Bedouins appeared at some distance in front, and created great alarm in our caravan. Our Sheik, or leader, had acquired, and deserved, the veneration and confidence of his followers, as much from his known prudence and valour, as from his dignity of Iman. He immediately ordered us to occupy the spot affording water, and himself, with about twenty Arabs and Tuaricks, advanced to reconnoitre the ground where the Bedouins had appeared : they had now retreated wholly out of sight, and we had time to cook and fill our water bags. We could not, however, consider this as a proper or safe station for the night; accordingly at four o'clock we proceeded on our march ; and about eight in the evening reached the foot of a sand-hill, and encamped in great disorder, created by the late alarm;—making no fires, and using every precaution to avoid notice or discovery of our retreat.

The next morning, September 8th, we entered the Desert, which may be considered as the boundary of Egypt; and after travelling thirteen hours, encamped on a tract of land by the Arabs called *Mubabag*.

The ensuing day, our journey was less fatiguing ; in four hours and a half we reached *Mogara*, a watering-place on the verge of a fruitful valley.

The water collected for the use of the caravans is carried in bags made of goat-skins, unripped in the middle, and stripped from the animal as entire as possible; those made at Soudan are the strongest and best; water may be preserved in them for five days, without acquiring any bad taste : the bags of an inferior manufacture give an ill taste, and a smell of the leather, from the second day. To render the skins flexible and lasting, they are greased on the inside with butter, and by the Arabs sometimes with oil, which latter gives quickly a rancid taste, and to any but an Arab, renders the water scarcely fit for drinking.

The sixth day we had again a difficult and tiresome journey of twelve hours, without halting; towards the close of our march, the horse of an Arab near me falling sick, and being unable to proceed at the same pace as the caravan, I kept in the rear to attend him, and give such assistance as might be required. On our coming up with the caravan at its evening encampment, the Arab immediately sent by his slave, two pieces of dried camel's flesh, with a proper compliment, requesting my acceptance of the present, as some return for the civility I had shewn. I was in an instant surrounded by a number of meaner Arabs, who eyed with avidity the meat I had received, and on my dividing it amongst them, seemed greatly surprised, that I should so readily part with what, in their estimation, was so great a dainty.

Circumstances light and trivial often delineate manners, and characterize nations : the method of equipment, and the means of sustenance which the Arab uses in journeying through these deserts, may furnish a subject of just curiosity, and certainly of special use to such as may undertake a similar expedition.

The Arab sets out on his journey with a provision of flour, kuskasa, onions, mutton suet, and oil or butter ; and some of the richer class add to this store, a proportion of biscuit, and of dried flesh. As soon as the camels are halted and the baggage unladen, the drivers and slaves dig a small hole in the sands wherein to make a fire, and then proceed in search of wood, and of three stones to be placed round the cavity, for the purpose of confining the embers and supporting the cauldron. The cauldron, (which is of copper,) being set over, the time till the water begins to boil is employed first in discussing, and then in preparing, what the mess of the day shall consist of. The ordinary meal is of *basside*, a stiff farinaceous pap, served up in a copper dish, which, in due economy of utensils and luggage, is at other times used for serving water to the camels : when this pap or pudding is thus served on table, it is diluted with a soup poured on it, enriched or seasoned with the *monachie* dried and finely pulverized. At other times, the dinner consists of flour kneaded into a strong dough, which being divided into small cakes and boiled, affords a species of hard dumplins called *mijotta*. A yet better repast is made of dried meat boiled together with mutton suet, onions sliced thin, crumbled biscuits, salt, and a good quantity of pepper. The meat is at dinner time taken out and reserved for the master, and the broth alone is the mess of his followers. The slaughtering of a camel affords a feast to the camel drivers and slaves. The friends of the owner of the beast have a preference in the purchase ; and after dividing the carcase, every slave comes in for a share : no part of the animal capable of being gnawed by human tooth, is suffered to be lost ; the very bones pass through various hands and mouths, before they are thrown away. They make sandals of the skin, and they weave the hair into twine.

It is not on every occasion that time can be allowed, or materials found, for dressing victuals : in the anticipation of such an exigency, the traveller provides a food called *simitée*: it consists of barley boiled until it swells, then dried in the sun, and then further dried over the fire ; and lastly, being ground into a powder, it is mixed with salt, pepper, and carraway-seed, and put into a leather bag : when it is to be used, it is kneaded into a dough, with just water enough to give it consistency, and is served up with butter or oil. If further diluted with water, then dates are added to the meal, and it is called *roum*. Such is the food of the traveller when there is a scarcity of fuel or of water ; and none can be expended in boiling. I was often, for days together, without other food than this cold farinaceous pap, mixed with a few dates. Onions and red Spanish pepper are the general and the only seasonings of each meal, with the addition of salt.

On the seventh day, after a march of four hours, we reached *Biljoradec*, commonly called *Jabudie*, a term implying that the water is bad, or that other water is not to be found but at a considerable distance.

The three following days, travelling occasionally in the night, we were forty hours in actual journey. On the first of these, (being the ninth day since leaving the vicinity of Cairo,) we reached the chain of mountains which bounded the uniform desert through which we had passed. On the tenth, mounting these hills, I observed the plain on their summit to consist of a saline mass spread over so large a tract of surface, that in one direction no eye could reach its termination, and what might be called its width, I computed at several miles. The clods of salt discoloured with sand lay thick and close, and gave to this vast plain the appearance of a recently ploughed field.

On the summit of this eminence, and almost in the middle of this saline tract, (on computation of its width) I discovered a spring; and the passage of Herodotus * occurring to my mind, in which he mentions springs of fresh water on the salt hills, I eagerly made up to its brink. I found it edged with salt: some poor pilgrims attending me tasted the water, but it was so saturated with saline matter, as to be wholly unfit for drink.

On the eleventh day (September the 15th), we came to an inhabited spot; after five hours march arriving at the small village of *Ummesogeir.*

* In hoc supercilio sunt frusta salis, ferè grumi grandes in colli'us, et singulorum collium vertices è medio sale ejaculantur aquam dulcem pariter et gelidam. Herodot. ed. Wesseling. p. 181.

## SECTION II.

*Observations on the Desert, from the Valley of Natron to the Mountains of Ummesogier.*

The Desert forms a natural boundary to Egypt, on the west extending from the *Natron Valley* to the mountains of *Ummesogier;* to the north, the dreary and barren plain is bounded by a chain of lofty hills, in view during the whole course of the caravan; and to the south, extends a journey, probably, of several days, by the ordinary mode of computation in these countries; but in this direction its limits are not defined, or are not known.

In this vast tract of sands, petrified wood is found, of various forms and size: sometimes are seen whole trunks of trees, of twelve feet circumference or more; sometimes only branches and twigs, scarcely of a quarter of an inch diameter; and sometimes merely pieces of bark of various kinds, and in particular of the oak, are to be found. Many of the great stems yet retain their side branches, and in many the natural timber has undergone so little change, that the circular ranges of the wood are discernible, and especially in those trunks which apparently were of oak. The interior of other bodies of timber was become a petrifaction, shewing no distinctions of grain or fibre, but bearing the appearance of mere stone; though the outward coat and form of the substance clearly denoted the tree.

Several Arabs informed me, that in travelling over this Desert, petrified trees were often found upright, and as if growing in the soil; but I presume, respecting those I did not see, from those I inspected, that they were merely trunks raised by hand, round the base of which the sand had quickly gathered before the winds, and formed a mound, as if heaved up by a root. The colour of the petrified wood is in general black, or nearly so; but in some instances it is of a light gray, and then so much resembling the wood in its natural state, that our slaves would often collect, and bring it in, for the purposes of firing.

These petrifactions are sometimes scattered in single pieces, but are oftener found in irregular layers, or strata, covering together a considerable space of ground.

If there yet remains any trace of a western branch of the Nile, as mentioned by ancient writers,* it is probably to be discovered in some part of this Desert. I observed no channel, or vestige of such course of river, on the route taken by the caravan. I would direct the researches of any future traveller specially to the tract of country round where we encamped on the nights when we halted at the foot of the sand hill west of *Wadey-el-Latron*, and in the district of *Muhabag:* these places we reached not till after sunset, and departing before day, I myself had no opportunity of examining the country. The term *Bahr-bella-ma*, commonly rendered *river without water*, by no means designates or points to any specific channel or tract in which any ancient channel may be more probably discovered: for if petrified trees fit for masts, or petrified timbers suited to other purposes of ship-building, said to be found in the

---

* Ῥέει γὰρ ἐκ Λιβύης ὁ Νεῖλος, καὶ μέσην τάμνων Λιβύην. Herodot. Euterpé, § 33. The Editor rather supposes that Herodotus using the term *Lybia*, comprised all Africa, west of Egypt and Ethiopia; and that the river, or branch of river, alluded to, is the great stream flowing from the west, described by the Nasamones, and supposed to be a part of the Nile, by Etearchus: in such case the traveller may in vain look for its channel in the country suggested by Mr. Horneman, it being undoubtedly far to the south,—the Joliba or Niger.

*Babr-bella-ma,* characterize and give the name (as we are told) to
the tract of land throughout which they are to be found, then the
appropriate translation is not river, but *sea without water,* for such
petrifactions are scattered over the whole Desert.  Indeed the general appearance of this vast and barren tract, well accords to the title
of *sea without water;* its sandy surface resembling that of a lee-
shore, over which the waters streaming before the storm have, on
their ebb, deposited timber, or what else was carried on by the tide.
I say not wreck of vessels, for I saw no wood that had the least
appearance of the tool, or of having been wrought for any purpose
of man.  Such as, by light observers, have been taken for fragments
of masts, are merely trunks of trees of from thirty to forty feet in
length, broken and shivered into large splinters, which lying near
each other, shew in their forms and grain of timber, the mass they
formerly belonged to and composed.

To the north of the Desert runs a chain of steep and bare calcareous mountains, which were in constant view of our caravan
travelling at the distance of three to seven miles in like direction.  At
the foot of these, runs a flat tract of moorish swampy land, from
one to six miles in breadth, abounding in springs, and to which we
resorted every second or third day for a supply of water; but at the
period of our journey, the springs throughout the whole valley were
nearly dried up.  The water which remained, and run or spread
on the surface, was *bitter;* \* yet digging wells near to these rivulets
or marshes, we found water at the depth only of five or six feet,
which was sweet and palatable.

---

\* So too Alexander, on his march to the Fane of Ammon, found the water *bitter :*
κατήυλησεν ἐπὶ ΠΙΚΡΑΝ καλυμένην λίμνην.

Did. Sic. Tom. I. p. 198, edit. Wesseling.

## SECTION III.

*Ummesogeir, and further Journey to Siwah.*

UMMESOGEIR is situated on a sandy plain stretching into the recess between two diverging branches of the mountain. In the valley thus formed, appear vast isolated masses of rock, on the largest of which the village is built; it is small, and contains few inhabitants, furnishing only thirty men capable of bearing arms. The houses are low, constructed of stones cemented with a calcareous earth, and thatched with the boughs of date trees. I was informed, that some of these buildings covered caves or chambers cut in the rock; probably ancient catacombs. Our camp was pitched at the foot of the rock, among date trees, through which the way leads up to the town. Its inhabitants, poor as they appeared, received us with hospitality; they came down, almost to a man, from their houses, and assisted us in watering our camels, or whatever service was required. Towards evening I walked up to the village by a path of very difficult access. Coming to a kind of market-place, in its centre I observed bargains making with such eagerness, noise, and altercation, that one should suppose the dealings to be of the first moment; but I soon perceived the sellers to be only a few poor pilgrims of our caravan, and their articles of trade to be merely *henna hoechel,* rings of lead or glass, and such like ornaments for women; which, with a little shot and gunpowder, they were bartering for dates : the merchandise on either side was not altogether worth a crown.

The people of Ummesogeir are indeed in every respect poor, depending wholly for subsistence on their dates, which they in part sell to the Arabs of the Desert, and in part carry to Alexandria, and exchange for corn, oil, or fat. Their manners are rude and simple, as might be expected, from a society so small, and separated from every other, by vast tracts of desert in every direction. Thus sequestered from the world, too weak in numbers for attack, and too poor to be attacked, these people derive, from their situation and habits of life, a simple and peaceful disposition. An old man told me, that the Bedouins once attempted to deprive them of their rock, and pittance which the date trees around furnished; and would have succeeded, had not a *marabut* (or holy man) who lies buried in the village, so dazzled the eyes of the invaders, that they could not find the place, though constantly roving round it. A like miracle was hoped for, and (in vain certainly) expected in favour of Cairo, when the French invaded Egypt. The idea of miraculous interposition of this kind appears to have been common to the Oriental nations.

During our stay at this place, the effects of a *Twater*, who died on the journey were sold by auction. Another man, during our route, was killed by a fall from his camel, pitching with his head on a pointed stone, and which caused his instant death. Two others, poor pilgrims from Mecca, fell victims to the fatigue and difficulties of so long a journey, and for which their scanty means were ill suited, either as to food or rest; and this completes our bill of mortality.

After some days of repose, we proceeded on our journey towards Siwah, distant from Ummesogeir a journey of twenty hours. We soon passed the skirts of the broad sandy plain, and reascended the mountains connected with, and stretching from, those which cover the vale of Ummesogeir to the west. A long and tedious passage over these hills led us finally to a green and fertile valley, towards which, as we descended from the mountain, we perceived people gathering provender for their cattle. Our train of heavy laden camels readily denoted that we were no troop of hostile Arabs; and the people leaving their work, ran to meet and congratulate us on our arrival. They told us that the whole neighbourhood was at peace, and that we might encamp safely and without apprehension. They mounted their asses and conducted us to a plain west of Siwah, and not far distant from that town, where we pitched our tents.

## SECTION IV.

### *Siwah.*

SIWAH is a small independent state ; it acknowledges, indeed, the grand Sultan paramount, but it pays him no tribute. Round its chief town called Siwah, are situated at one or two miles distance, the villages of *Scharkie,* (in Siwahian dialect termed *Agrmie,*) *Msellem, Monachie, Sbocka,* and *Barischa.* Siwah is built upon, and round, a mass of rock ; in which, according to tradition, the ancient people had only caves for their habitation. Indeed the style of building is such, that the actual houses might be taken for caves; they are raised so close to each other, that many of the streets, even at noon, are dark, and so intricate, that a stranger cannot find his way into or out of the town, small as it is, without a guide. Many of the houses built on the declivity of the rock, and especially those terminating the descent towards the plain, are of more than ordinary height, and their walls particularly thick and strong, so as to form a circumvallation of defence to the town within.

The people of our caravan compared Siwah to a bee-hive, and the comparison is suitable, whether regarding the general appearance of the eminence thus covered with buildings, the swarm of its people crowded together, or the confused noise, or hum and buz from its narrow passages and streets, and which reach the ear to a considerable distance.

Round the foot of the eminence are erected stables for the

camels, horses, and asses, which could not ascend to, or could not be accommodated in, the town above.

The territory of SiwAH is of considerable extent;* its principal and most fruitful district is a well watered valley of about fifty miles in circuit, hemmed in by steep and barren rocks. Its soil is a sandy loam, in some places rather poached or fenny; but, assisted by no great industry of the natives, it produces corn, oil, and vegetables for the use of man or beast : its chief produce, however, consists in dates, which, from their great quantity and excellent flavour, render the place proverbial for fertility among the surrounding Arabs of the Desert. Each inhabitant possesses one or more gardens, making his relative wealth ; and these it is his whole business to water and cultivate. A large garden yielding all such produce as is natural to the country, is valued at the price of from four to six hundred im-perial dollars, there termed *real-patuacks.* The gardens round the towns or villages, are fenced with walls from four to six feet high, and sometimes with hedges ; they are watered by many small streams of salt or sweet water, falling from the bordering rocks and mountains, or issuing from springs rising in the plain itself, and which, for the purposes of irrigation, being diverted into many small channels, expend themselves in the vale, and in no instance flow beyond the limits of this people's territory. The dates pro-duced are preserved in public magazines, of which the key is kept by the Sheik : to these storehouses the dates are brought in baskets closely rammed down, and a register of each deposit is kept.

North-west of Siwah, there is a stratum of salt extending a full mile, and near it salt is found on the surface, lying in clods or small lumps. On this spot rise numerous springs, and frequently a spring

* Vide Note, Appendix, No. I.

of water perfectly sweet is found within a few paces from one which is salt. North of Siwah, on the road leading to *El-Mota*, I found many of these salt springs quite close to others which were sweet.

It is not easy to ascertain the general population of a place, with so little police, and so little regularity of government as Siwah, unless opportunity occurred of seeing its people assembled at some general meeting or festival. The number of its warriors, however, is more easily known ; and on such data, further estimate of its population may be made. According to the ancient constitution and laws of the state, the government should be vested in twelve Sheiks, two of whom were to administer its powers in rotation ; but a few years past, twenty other wealthy citizens, forced themselves into a share of authority, assumed the title of Sheik, and enlarging the circle of aristocracy, increased the pretensions and disputes for power. On each matter of public concern, they now hold general councils. I attended several of these general meetings, held close to the town wall, where the chiefs were squatted in state ; and I observed, that a strong voice, violent action, great gesticulation, abetted by party support and interest, gained the most applause, and carried the greatest influence: perhaps such result is not uncommon in most popular meetings. Whenever these councils cannot agree ultimately on any point, then the leaders and people fly to arms, and the strongest party carries the question. Justice is administered according to ancient usage, and general notions of equity. Fines, to be paid in dates, constitute the punishments : for instance, the man who strikes another, pays from ten to fifty *kaftas* or baskets of dates ; these baskets, by which every thing in this place is estimated and appraised, are about three feet high, and four in circumference.

The dress of the men consists of a white cotton shirt and breeches, and a large calico cloth, striped white and blue, (manufactured at Cairo,) which is folded and thrown over the left shoulder, and is called *melaye*. On their heads they wear a cap of red worsted or cotton. These caps, chiefly made at Tunis, are a covering, characteristic of the Mussulman ; and no Jew or Christian on the coasts of Barbary is permitted to wear them. At times of festival, the Siwahans dress themselves in *kaftans* and a *benisch*, such as the Arabs commonly wear when in towns.

The women of Siwah wear wide blue shifts, usually of cotton, which reach to the ankles, and a *melaye* (as above described), which they wrap round their head, from which it falls over the body in manner of a cloak.

They plait their hair into three tresses, one above the other; in the lowermost tress they insert various ornaments of glass, or false coral, or silver, and twist in long stripes of black leather, hanging down the back, and to the ends of which they fasten little bells. On the crown of their heads, they fix a piece of silk or woollen cloth, which floats behind. As ear-rings they wear two, and some women three, large silver rings, inserted as links of a chain : their necklace is glass imitating coral ; those of the higher class wear round their necks a solid ring of silver, somewhat thicker than the collar usually worn by criminals in some parts of Europe ; from this ring, by a chain of the same metal, hangs pendant a silver plate, engraved with flowers and other ornaments, in the Arabian taste. They further decorate their arms and legs, (just above the ancle,) with rings of silver, of copper, or of glass.

I can give no favourable account of the character of the people of

Siwah, either from general repute, or from my own observation. I
found them obtrusive and thievish. Our tents, and especially my
own, were constantly surrounded and infested by this people ; and
our merchants were under the necessity of guarding their bales of
goods, with more than ordinary attention, under apprehension not
merely of pillage, but of general and hostile attack.

I was told much of the riches of this people, and should suppose
there must be men of considerable property amongst them ; as they
have a very extensive traffic in dates with different and remote
countries, pay no tribute, and have little opportunity of dissipating
the money they receive. The policy of the Siwahans leads them to
cultivate a strict and close amity with the Arabs to the north of their
country, and who occasionally visit Siwah in small troops or parties,
and carry on a trade of barter for the dates. Here our caravan disposed of part of its merchandize, receiving in exchange, dates, meat,
and small baskets, in the weaving and context of which, the
women of Siwah are remarkably neat and skilful, and in the making of which consists their chief employment. Diseases incident to
the country and climate, and from which the natives most suffer,
are the ague and fever, and opthalmic affections, or disorders of
the eyes.

The language of Siwah, whatever words or expressions may have
crept in, from various intercourse of people, is not fundamentally
Arabic; and this has led me to various conjectures. At first I looked
for the root or origin of this language to the East; but on maturer
consideration, and from communications with one of the *Tuaricks*
from *Twat*, with whom I was in habits of intimacy, I am now
satisfied of my former error,* and that the language of Siwah is a

* Vide Appendix, No. IV.

dialect of that used throughout the great nation of Africa, to which my friend, the Tuarick, belonged, and which may be considered as the aboriginal.

The larger collection of Siwahan words, which I had first made, was lost with other papers, by an accident which I shall hereafter have occasion to mention.

The following list I had from a man of Siwah, whom I afterwards got acquainted with at Augila.

| | | | |
|---|---|---|---|
| Sun, | *Itfuct.* | Horse, | *Achmar.* |
| Clouds, | *Logman.* | Horses, | *Ickmare.* |
| Far, | *Temmesocht.* | Have you a horse? | *Goreck Achmar.* |
| Head, | *Achfé.* | Milk, | *Achi.* |
| Eye, | *Taun.* | Fennel, | *Acksum.* |
| Eyelid, | *Temauin.* | Bread, | *Tagora.* |
| Beard, | *Itmert.* | Oil, | *Tsemur.* |
| Hand, | *Fuss.* | Water, | *Aman.* |
| Penis, | *Achmum.* | Dates, | *Tena.* |
| Camel, | *Lgum.* | House, | *Achbén.* |
| Sheep, | *Jelibb.* | Houses, | *Gebeun.* |
| Cow, | *Ftunest.* | Sand, | *Itjeda.* |
| Mountain, | *Iddrarn.* | Cap, | *Tschatschet.* |
| Sabre, | *Aus.* | Catacombs, | *Tum-megar.* |
| Sword, | *Limscha.* | | |

## SECTION V.

*Antiquities of Siwah.*

As we approached the spot destined for our encampment in the
Vale of Siwah, I descried to the westward some ruins of an extensive building, a few miles distant from the road, and concluded them
to be the same as noticed by a late English traveller, (Mr. Brown,)
of whose discoveries I heard first in London, and afterwards, when
in Egypt. Circumstances rendered it necessary for me to be particularly on my guard, and to defer any visit to, or actual inspection
of, these antiquities, until I had retrieved the confidence of the
natives, who, on my very first appearance, (as I was informed,)
had taken me and my interpreter, for Christians; and to this supposition they were induced, from our fairer complexion, from our
gait and manners, and from our Turkish dresses. When I took
advantage of the disturbances at Cairo and its environs, to get introduced as a Mahomedan to the caravan, I could not indeed speak
readily, either Turkish or Arabic ; but in this, I flattered myself,
the assumed character of a young Mameluke might be my excuse;
and I further derived confidence from the experience and abilities
of my interpreter, who (a German by birth,) had been forced,
twelve years past, to embrace the Mahommedan religion at Con-
stantinople, and whose address and knowledge, I hoped, might
preclude, or extricate me from, any consequences of jealousy or
suspicion.

Considering the importance of my mission, and the great purpose
of exploring the whole of Northern Africa, with which I was

entrusted, perhaps it had been more wise and prudent on my part, not to have exposed myself to general intercourse, until better qualified to sustain the character I had assumed; had I so done in the present instance, and abstained from visiting the curiosities of Siwah, and exposing myself in the novelty of the attempt, to examinations and suspicions, I might have avoided a danger which (as will appear in the sequel) nearly proved fatal to myself, and therewith to the object of my voyage.

Making such candid admission of not having the requisite forbearance, with objects of so just curiosity in view, I proceed to state the course of my inquiries, and the result.

I first visited the ruins of the extensive edifice before observed. I accosted some men working in the gardens near, and questioning them as to what they knew of this building, they answered, " that in former times Siwah was inhabited by infidels, most of whom lived in caves, but some inhabited these buildings." One spokesman, pointing to a building in the centre, said, " tradition tells us, *that edifice* was the hall in which the divan used to assemble; at time of its construction men were stronger than I am; for those huge stones serving as a roof to the fabric, were lifted up and placed there by two men only: there is much gold buried under the walls." When I then entered into the ruins, I was followed by all the people near, and thus prevented examining the place with any accuracy. On a second visit I was not more successful; and when, after a few days, I returned thither again, some Siwahans directly said to me, " thou undoubtedly art yet a Christian in thy heart, else why come so often to visit these works of Infidels." In order to maintain the character I had assumed, I was thus necessitated to abandon any further project of nice examination or admeasurement, and restrict myself to general observations, such as I now submit in detail as they occurred.

*Ummebeda* (the name given to the site of those ruins by the natives) lies near a village called *Scharkie* or *Agrmie*, between that place and an isolated mountain, on which a copious spring of fresh water is said to rise. The buildings are in such a state of delapidation, that a plain observer, who forms an opinion only from what he sees, and does not accommodate the object in application and conjecture to preconceived notions of a particular structure which he is to look for, and trace out, could scarcely, (I think) from these rude heaps, and mouldered and disjointed walls, suggest the precise form or original purpose of the building when first raised. Its materials might suggest, that it was built in the rudest ages, and when the Troglodytæ* of these parts first left their caves, and in their first attempt of building, took their scheme and plan of architecture from their old mansions, heaping rock on rock, in imitation of the dwelling places which nature had before furnished.

I ascertained the general bearings of the building by my compass, and found the outward walls constructed with aspects facing the four cardinal points, the aberration being only of twelve degrees, and which might have occurred from variation of the needle. The total circumference may be several hundred yards, and is to be traced out and followed by the foundations of a wall, in most parts visible, and which, from the masses remaining, appears to have been *very strong*. The outward wall, in most places, has been thrown down, and the materials carried away, and the interior ground has been every where turned up, and dug, in search of treasure.

* Vide Herodot. edit. Wesseling, p. 284.

In the centre of this extensive area, are seen the remains of an edifice, which perhaps may be regarded as the principal building,* and to which all around may have been mere appendage, and subordinate.

The northern part of this building stands on a native calcareous rock, rising above the level of the general area, within the outer walls, about eight feet. The height of the edifice appears to be about twenty-seven feet; its width twenty-four, and its length ten or twelve paces. The walls are six feet in thickness, the exterior of which within and without is constructed of large free stones, filled up in the interstice with small stones and lime. The ceiling is formed by vast blocks of stone, wrought and fitted to stretch over and cover the entire building. The breadth of each such mass of stone is about four feet, and the depth or thickness three feet. One of these stones of the roof has fallen in, and is broken; the entire southern wall of the building hath likewise tumbled, and the materials have mostly been carried away. But the people have not been able to remove the large fragments fallen from the roof, which their ancestors were enabled to bring from the quarry, and to raise entire to the summit of the edifice. Such are the vicissitudes of art, of knowledge, and of human powers and means, as well as of human happiness and fortunes!

The stones that have fallen, lie sunk, with their surface lower than the base of the yet standing part of the building, and their bottom almost on a level with the area of the great inclosure. The appearance of these fallen stones of the southern wall, leads to a conjecture, that this extremity of the original edifice had its floor or base *lower than that of the northern part.* The entrances to this

* Vide Note, Appendix, No. I.

building are three, the principal one to the north, and the others to
the east and west. The inside walls (beginning at half their height
from the ground) are decorated with hieroglyphics sculptured in
relief, but the figures seem not to have been sufficiently engraved
in *alt*, or *salient*, to resist the ravages of time and weather; and in
some places they are wholly mouldered and defaced, and especially
on the ceiling.

On different parts of the wall appear marks of paint, and the
colour seems to have been green. I could no where discover traces
of the edifice having in any part been lined or inlaid with a finer
stone or material. A few paces from the chief entrance, I observed
two round stones, of about three feet diameter, each indented, as if
to receive the base of some statue or other ornament. The general
material of which the building is constructed, is a lime-stone, containing petrifactions of shells and small marine animals; and such
stone is to be found and dug up in the vicinity.

On examining the country around these ruins, I found the soil
contiguous to the foundations of the outward wall on the south to
be marshy, and was informed that it contained salt springs. I asked
if no considerable spring of fresh water was to be seen near; and
was shewn a fine rivulet of sweet water, about half a mile from the
ruins, which takes its rise in a grove of date trees, and in a most
romantic and beautiful situation : it is not, however, its delightful
scene that recommends it to the native of Siwah, but an opinion
that it is a specific against certain diseases.

I am conscious that the above description of the remains of antiquity near Siwah, is by far too cursory and incomplete, for any
purpose of just and accurate inference; and that it must yet remain

a mere conjecture, whether these ruins are those of the famous *Temple of Jupiter Ammon*. It must be obvious, from many points I have adverted to in my description, that I had the site of this renowned temple in view, and that it was a principal object of my research. Circumstances I was under, and of which the reader is already apprised, prevented my pursuing this great subject of just and learned curiosity with the nicety of inspection, and care in the consideration, which I could have wished to employ. Supposing, on reference to ancient writers, the comparison of the buildings not to bear me out in the idea which I entertain ; yet on many other grounds I should contend, that Siwah had been a residence of the ancient Ammonites. I draw my conclusion from the relative situation of the country ; from the quality of the soil, from its fertility; from the information of its inhabitants, that no other such fruitful tract is to be found any where near ; and, in addition to the certainty, at least, that some great and magnificent building once here stood, I derive a further conclusion from the numerous catacombs to be found in the vicinity, and which I shall have occasion more particularly to notice. In regard to the memorable Temple of Ammon, should even my own description of the existing vestiges of building not accurately agree with general accounts of that edifice, yet, notwithstanding, I must continue to hold an opinion, from the general appearance and from the situation of those ruins, that they *may be* remains of the *Temple of Jupiter Ammon*. A delineation and decipher of the hieroglyphic figures, which adorn the inner walls of the building, might be conclusive on this question.

I will further add on this subject, that on inquiry after *Edrisi's Santrich*, no one knew it even by name; but I was told that at a distance of seven days journey from *Siwah*, six from *Faiume*, and

two or three\* from *Biljoradec*, there exists a country, similar to that
of Siwah, its inhabitants less in number, and speaking the same
language. That region I should take to be the *Minor Oasis* of the
ancients. I speak of this place from mere report, and could gain
no more accurate, or further account; perhaps it lies among the
mountains which traverse the great Desert near *Ummesogeir*, extending towards the south.

I come now to the subject of the *various catacombs*, to be found
in the territory of Siwah, and which I was enabled more fully to
examine, as lying in more sequestered spots, and where I was less
liable to observation.

If I well understood my companion, an inhabitant of Siwah, there
are four principal places, where catacombs are found. The first,
*Belled-el-Kaffer;* the second, *Belled-el-Rumi ;* both these terms,
denote one and the same thing, namely, " place or town of infidels ;"
the third is, *El-Mota*, or place of burial ; the fourth, *Belled-el-Chamis*,
or *Gamis.* My inquiries were in particular directed to *El-Mota*,
situated at the distance of about one mile north-east from Siwah. It
is a rocky hill, with a number of catacombs on the declivity, but the
most remarkable, are on the summit. There is a separate entrance
to each, and the descent inwards is gentle and gradual. The passage
from the aperture, leads to a door-way, from which the space of the
room is enlarged, and on each side, are smaller excavations for containing the mummies. The stones rising from the threshold are
cut in a form that shews a door to have been formerly hung, and
to have closed the entrance. The catacombs are of different extent,
and each is wrought with great labour and neatness of work, and
especially the uppermost, which contains no traces of any mummy.

\* The distance from Biljoradec is not clearly expressed in the original.

In others are found various remains. I long, but in vain, searched for an entire head: I found fragments, and especially of the *occiput* in abundance, but none with any investiture remaining; and even in the *occiputs* most entire I could not discover any stain or mark of their once having been filled with *resin*. The cloth still adhered to some *ribs*, but so decayed, that nothing could be further distinguished, than that the stuff in which the mummy had been wrapt, was of the coarsest kind.

The ground in all these catacombs has been dug and explored in search of treasure, and I was told, by my guide, that in every one of these sepulchres gold has been, and is yet sometimes, found.

There is every probability that entire mummies might be discovered in the catacombs at a greater distance to *westward* of Siwah. I was credibly informed, that besides the open catacombs on the mountains, there are others under ground, and the entrance of which is to be found at no great depth; and that *Biut-el-Nazari*, (houses of Christians, synonymous here to Infidels,) exist on both sides of a long subterraneous passage, forming a communication, between two catacomb-mountains. The catacombs met with on *Gibel-el-belled*, being the hill on which *Siwah* is built, are small, and consist of a little antichamber, leading generally to two caverns where the mummies were deposited. Of these the two most remarkable are two large and high caverns on the north side; the one is twenty, the other sixteen feet square, and both are open to the north.

There are likewise two other caverns, of similar dimensions, but not so lofty, to be seen westward of *Siwah*, and leading to *Augila*;

their entrance is low and narrow, and the two excavations are so near, that the partition, as appears from a small perforation, is only ten inches thick.

Quitting the subject of antiquities in the territory of Siwah, I have only to add, that in the nearest plain west of the town, there are other massive remains of some building, but which bear no token or note of remote antiquity, such as may be attributed to the ruins I first described.

## SECTION VI.

*Departure from Siwah.—Journey to Schiacha, and Danger which
the Traveller there incurred.*

HAVING remained eight days at Siwah; on the 29th of September,
at three in the afternoon, we broke up our encampment, and proceeded a three hours march, when we again pitched our tents at
foot of a hill. The next day we began our journey late, being delayed till one o'clock, in search of a slave who belonged to a court-
officer of the Sultan of Fezzan, and who had absconded from the
caravan. Whilst the man was looking for, I set out with a view of
inspecting some catacombs which I descried on the neighbouring
hills, but was stopped at some distance by a lake of seven or eight
miles in circumference, formed at the base of the mountain by the
conflux of springs and small pools of water, which the rains at this
season had swollen and brought together. Returning to the camp,
I took my telescope to examine the appearances I was not enabled
closely to inspect, when the first object on the mountain which presented itself to my view was the Negro after whom the search was
making. I gave no notice of my discovery, the poor fellow having
a good character, and having been driven to the attempt of flight by
the extreme severity of his master. I am sorry to say there was
little hope of his final escape, the Siwahans having promised to
deliver him up. This day we travelled till half an hour after sunset. The next day we marched at two hours before day-break, and
halted at nine. The fourth day brought us to the fruitful valley of
*Schiacha.*

The mountains by which we travelled from *Siwah* to this spot, are branches of those which I have mentioned as appearing, at all times, to north of our way through the Desert, and often at but little distance. They rise abruptly, and as precipices, from the level ground, and shew a face of mere rock, without the least covering of soil or even of sand. Their appearance, taken together with that of the *sea-sand* which covers the Desert, indicate this vast tract to have been flooded, and at a period later than the great deluge. In the sandy plain below these mountains is seen the surface of a vast calcareous rock, containing no substance of petrifaction, whereas the mountains near consist of limestone, crowded and filled with fragments of marine animals and shells. The strata of all these rocky hills lay horizontal.

Westward of *Siwah*, I found two banks or heaps of calcined shells, some of the size of two inches over. My interpreter told me, that taking his road at some distance from me, he saw a mountain standing singly and unconnected with others, composed entirely of shells. Many such vast isolated mounds are to be seen throughout the whole of this district, and the bed-joints or interstices of their strata of stone (always horizontal), being filled up with a reddish, friable, calcareous substance, they often resemble pyramids, and in so exact and illusive a manner, that more than once I was deceived into expectation of arrival at such building. The architecture of the ancient Egyptians was of the vast and gigantic kind; and builders of such ambitious temper and stupendous scheme, might readily entertain the idea of transforming a mountain into a pyramid, shaping the huge rock, already in form partly adapted, and casing it with wrought stones on the outside, as they might prefer. Some of the learned have given an opinion, that the Pyramids of *Giza* and of *Saccara*, were not originally erections from the base, but merely hills of earth or stone, shaped and covered by the labour of man. The idea is plausible, though certainly to be controverted, by reasons to be drawn from history, and from other the best sources of fact and argument.

I now proceed to the recital of an event in which I was personally and principally concerned. I shall give the recital in detail, as, in its consequences, being of the highest import to the future safety of myself, and therewith to the progress of discovery which I have engaged in ; and, as it has afforded me self-confidence and new encouragement, ever favourable to the success of enterprize, so will it, I trust, give satisfaction to those who have employed me, inspiring just and well-founded hopes of my finally accomplishing the great purpose entrusted to my care.

The state of quiet and security usually attending our encampments was interrupted, whilst at *Schiacha*, by the arrival of some Siwahans, who, about eight o'clock in the evening, came with intelligence, that a numerous horde of Arabs from the vicinity of *Faiume* were hovering in the Desert, ready to fall upon our caravan. These messengers at the same time assured us, that the people of Siwah had resolved to come to our assistance, and to escort us to the next watering-place; adding, " that their little army would arrive in a few hours, determined to risk with us every thing in opposing the attack of the Bedouins, whose force they represented as consisting of from 800 to 1000 men. Our leader, the Sheik of the Twaters, immediately assembled the principal people of the caravan, when it was decided not to desert our post, but to await the enemy. Scarcely was our little council broke up, when we heard from afar the braying of some hundred asses, giving notice of the approach of the *Siwahans*. They use this animal on their military excursions, from

the advantage it affords of more easily proceeding by narrow and
rugged passes among the mountains, and evading or attacking any
enemy, who from ignorance of the country, or from the nature of
its cattle requiring safer roads, is obliged to confine its march to
broader defiles or vallies.   Some men were immediately dispatched
from the caravan, requiring the Siwahans to halt at half a mile
distance from our post.   The night passed in disquietude and alarm :
each got his arms in readiness, and prepared for a battle on the
ensuing day.   A little before sun-rise, the Siwahans advanced on
foot, and gave apprehension of immediate attack.   Some *Augilans*
rode forward, to inquire their intentions, and were answered, " that
the caravan had nothing to fear :" on reporting this to the Sheik,
he sent the messengers back, to say he should consider and treat
them as enemies, if they advanced a step further.   On this message
the *Siwahans* halted, formed a circle, and invited some *Augilans* to
a conference.   During all this time, I remained quiet with my baggage, having sent my interpreter to collect intelligence of what was
passing.   Seeing him return, and judging from his manner and
haste, that he had something of importance to communicate, I ran
to meet him.   He immediately accosted me with, " cursed be the
moment, when I determined upon this journey ; we are both of us
unavoidably lost men ; they take us for Christians and spies, and
will assuredly put us to death."   With these words he left me, and
ran to the baggage, where he exchanged his single gun for my
double barrelled one, and armed himself with two brace of pistols.
I upbraided him with his want of firmness, told him " a steady and
resolute conduct could alone preserve ourselves and friends, and
reminded him that his present behaviour was precisely such as to
give weight to the suspicions entertained :" I further urged, " that
on his own account he had nothing to fear, having for twelve
years been a Mahommedan, and perfectly acquainted with the

religion and customs ; that myself alone was in danger, and that I hoped to avert it, provided *he* did not intermeddle with my defence." " Friend, (answered he,) you will never hear of danger: but this time you will pay for your temerity."

Perceiving that terror had wholly deprived him of the necessary temper and recollection, I now left him to himself, and walked up unarmed, but with a firm and manly step, to this tumultuous assembly.

I entered the circle, and offered the Mahometan salutation,. " *Assulam Alckum*," but none of the *Siwahans* returned it. Some of them immediately exclaimed,—" You are of the new Christians from Cairo, and come to explore our country." Had I at this time, been as well acquainted with Mahometan fanaticism, and the character of the Arabs, as I have been since, I should have deduced my defence from the very terms of the accusation, and stated that I was indeed from Cairo, having fled from the Infidels ; as it was, I answered nothing to this general clamour, but sat down and directed my speech to one of the Chiefs, whose great influence I knew, and who had been often in my tent whilst at *Siwah*. " Tell me, brother. (said I,) hast thou ever before known 300 armed men take a journey of three days, in pursuit of two men, who dwelt in their *midst* for ten days, who had eaten and drank with them as friends, and whose tents were open to them all ? Thyself hast found us praying and reading the Koran ; and now thou sayest we are Infidels from Cairo ; *that is,* one of those from whom we fly ! Dost thou not know, that it is a great sin to tell one of the faithful that he is a Pagan ?" I spoke this with an earnest and resolute tone, and many of the congregation seemed gained over by it, and disposed to be favourable to me : the man replied, " that he was convinced we

were not Infidels, that he had persuaded no one to this pursuit, and
as far as depended on him alone, he was ready to return to *Siwah*."
On this I turned to one of the vulgar, who was communicating
some of the accusations against me to the people of our caravan.
" Be thou silent, (said I,) would to God, that I were able to speak well
the Arabic, I would then ask questions of thee, and of hundreds like
thee, who are less instructed in the *Islam* than I am." An old man
on this observed, " This man is younger than the other, and yet
more courageous !" I immediately continued, " My friend is not
afraid of thee, but thou oughtest to have fears of my friend : dost
thou know what it is to reproach a man, who lives with sultans and
with princes, with being an Infidel ?" I was then asked for what
purpose we carried Christian papers. I now found that my interpreter had unwarily shewn a passport which I had obtained from
General Bonaparte, with a view not to be detained at the French
posts through which I was to pass to the caravan. My interpreter
at this moment came up, and finding me alive, and the assembly
less angry and violent, than when on being first questioned, he had
exasperated them by inconsiderate and perplexed answers; he recovered himself, and stood sufficiently composed and collected, whilst
I explained partly in German, partly in Arabic, what had passed.
Knowing, however, that the paper in question would be demanded,
and not choosing to trust to his prudence in the manner of producing
it ; I went myself for it to the tent, and returning, brought likewise
a Koran with me. I immediately tendered the paper to a Chief of
the *Siwahans*, who having unfolded it, asked, " if any by-stander
could read it." I could not help smiling at the question, perilous
as was my situation. The same question was then put to us, when
I answered, " that we did not understand what it contained, but
were told, it would allow us to quit Cairo without being molested."
" This is the book, (interrupted my interpreter,) which I under-

stand :" and immediately took the Koran from my hand. We were ordered, by reading in it, to give proof of our being truly of the religion. Our learning in this respect went far indeed beyond the simple ability of reading. My companion knew the entire Koran by heart, and as for me, I could even then write Arabic, and well too: which with these people, was an extraordinary proficiency in learning. We had scarcely given a sample of our respective talents, when the chiefs of our caravan, who to this moment had been silent, now took loudly our part; and many of the Siwahans too, interfered in our favour. In short, the inquiry ended to our complete advantage, though not without the murmuring of some in the multitude, who lost the hopes of plunder which the occasion might have afforded.

Thus the character of Mussulman which I assumed was firmly established, and I shall not be subjected in future, to like inquiries, on which, perhaps, more decisive proofs might be required, and which I could not give. The security of my future voyage is thus assured, and so great an advantage more than compensates for some losses attending the above incident, but which yet I must regret.

During the time I was first in conference with the people of Siwah, and those of the caravan, my baggage was left with my interpreter; who in the paroxysms of his fears, and indeed with no light apprehensions of our bales of goods being searched, took my remains of mummies, my specimens of mineralogy, my *more detailed* remarks, made on my way from Cairo to *Schiacha*, and generally my books, and gave them to a confidential slave of my Arab inmate, to bury them in a bog; this was done, and I never afterwards could retrieve them.

## SECTION VII.

*Departure from Schiacha—arrival at Augila.*

On the fifth day (reckoning by our departure from Siwah,) we left Schiacha, and travelled about four hours, when we encamped. The next morning in two hours and a half, we came to a district called *Torfauc,* where we halted to collect fresh water : from this place we departed at four in the afternoon of the same day, and continued our march until eight the next morning, through a desert, the level of which was interrupted by numerous sand-hills ; at eight o'clock we stopped to refresh, and rested till two o'clock, when we again pressed forward, and continued our march till eight in the morning, when we encamped till one. At one we again proceeded, travelled all night, and till three o'clock the next morning, when the party with whom I travelled, discovered, that during the night, we had wandered from the caravan ; we resolved thereon to halt and await the return of day. We placed our baggage by the side of each camel, to be enabled on emergency, to load again with dispatch, and I laid me down to sleep on the sand, with the bridle in one hand, and my firelock in the other, and slept soundly till sunrise.

We now discovered our caravan ; and at the same time, that we were not above half a mile from a spot, fruitful and abounding in water. We immediately made up to the place and encamped. The journey from *Torfauc* to this spot, was the most disagreeable and fatiguing that in the course of all my travels I had experienced. Both men and cattle were so wearied and exhausted, that as soon as the baggage was unladen, all resorted to sleep. We here reposed the whole day, and the next set forth for Augila, by short marches, (altogether not amounting to more than nine hours travel); we used no haste, as having nothing to apprehend, being now in the country of our friends.

Our entry into *Mojabra*, one of the three places belonging to the dominion of Augila, was solemn and affecting, as the greater part of the merchants of our caravan had here habitations and families. The Bey of *Bengasi*, Vicegerent for the Bashaw of *Tripoly*, and at that time resident at *Augila*, sent about twenty of his Arabs to note in writing the burden of the camels, and for which they demanded a small duty. These Arabs then ranged themselves, and formed a right wing to our caravan, drawn up for procession  The merchants who had horses formed the left, and the pilgrims and ordinary Arabs formed the centre, headed by the Sheik preceded by a green flag. The pilgrims marched on singing; and the Arabs made their horses prance and curvet, and so continued until we approached near to *Mojabra;* where a number of old men and children met us, to felicitate and get a first embrace of their sons and relations, whom, on hearing of the French invasion in Egypt, they had given over as lost.

We pitched our tents in a spot adjoining the town, and were most hospitably entertained. The following night I proceeded on my journey towards *Augila*, in company with two merchants, one of whom procured me a lodging on my arrival, it being the intention of the caravan to stop longer than usual at this place.

There are three towns within the territory of *Augila;* Augila, the capital, and *Mojabra*, and *Meledila.* The two last are near to each other, and both about four hours from Augila ; *Mojabra* to the south, and *Meledila* to north of the road by which we passed. *Mojabra* and *Meledila* are occasionally comprehended in the general name of *Fallo*, designating the district.

*Augila*, a town well known in the time of Herodotus,* covers a space of about one mile in circumference. It is badly built, and the streets are narrow and not kept clean. The houses are built of a limestone, dug from the neighbouring hills, and consist only of one story or ground floor. The apartments are dark, there being no aperture for light but the door ; and are generally ranged round a small court, to which the entrance of each room faces, for purpose of collecting the more light. The public buildings, comparatively, are yet more mean and wretched. *Mojabra* is of smaller extent, but appears proportionally more populous than *Augila* The inhabitants of *Meledila* are chiefly employed in agriculture; those of *Mojabra* engage mostly in trade, and pass their lives in travelling betwixt Cairo and Fezzan. The people of *Augila* are of a more sedentary disposition; though some of these too, were with our caravan.

The men of the above places, who engage in the caravan trade, generally keep three houses ; one at *Kardaffi*, near Cairo ; one at *Mojabra*, and a third at *Zuila*, or sometimes at *Mourzouk*. Many have a wife and family establishment at each of these houses; and others take a wife for the time, if the stay of the caravan is longer than usual. The men from their very youth devote themselves to such traveller's life. Boys from thirteen to fourteen years of age, accompanied our caravan the long and toilsome journey from *Augila*

---

* Herodotus places Augila at *ten* days journey from the city of the Ammonians. Melpom. 182. N. B. Mr. Horneman was *nine* days on journey from Augila to Siwah, partly by forced marches.

to *Fezzan* on foot, or at least seldom mounting a horse. In observing the general character of this people, I could not but remark a degradation, self-interestedness, and mean and shuffling disposition, derived from early habits of petty trade, and the manner in which it was conducted, as contra-distinguishing those engaged in this traffic, and those who remained at home.

The men of the country are engaged in gardening and agriculture; but in the last to no great extent. The women are very industrious in manufacturing coarse woollen cloths of five yards in length and a yard and a half wide, which are called *Abbe*, and are sent in considerable quantities to *Fezzan*. These constitute the chief clothing of this people; they wrap them about their bodies, and without even a shirt or shift under.

Round *Augila* the country is level and the soil sandy, yet, being well watered, is tolerably fertile. Corn is not cultivated in quantity sufficient for subsistence of the people. The Arabs of *Bengasi*, distant about thirteen days journey, import annually both wheat and barley; and this their corn caravan is generally accompanied by flocks of sheep for sale.

The inhabitants of this region can generally speak the *Arabic*, but their vulgar language is a dialect similar to that of Siwah, above noticed.

# CHAPTER II.

## SECTION I.

*Augila, to the Confines of Temissa.*

Soon after our arrival at *Augila*, a man was sent off by the chief of the caravan to examine the watering-places as far the borders of the kingdom of Fezzan. This precaution became necessary from the increased number of people and camels, now forming this great caravan, and the possibility that, from want of rain or other causes, the springs on the usual route might not afford sufficient water for so large a body. The messenger being ordered to use the utmost dispatch, returned on the twelfth day with the happy intelligence, that water was in plenty, and that he met with nothing to impede our journey.

Accordingly, the 27th of October was the day fixed for our departure from *Augila*, and myself and party quitted the town the preceding evening, and encamped in the open air, to be among the first at the breaking up and movement of the caravan. The next morning we set out before sunrise, and proceeded in a direction west by south. Our caravan was increased by companies of merchants from *Bengasi*, *Merote*, and *Mojabra*, in all about 120 men. Many of the inhabitants of *Augila* and *Fallo*, accompanied us part of the way, and, as a mark of honour and attention, pranced their horses and fired their muskets round us. This party had scarcely taken their leave, when an Arab riding to us in haste, gave information, that we were pursued by a large body of horse, and that they were even then close upon our rear. On this intelligence the camels were immediately driven by the slaves and boys to a rising ground, and those who had arms mustered to cover the retreat, and prevent the enemy's irruption and pillage. At the moment we were preparing for action, we were happily undeceived. The horsemen were troops of the Bey of *Bengasi* (then resident at Augila as I before mentioned), and who, hearing the complimentary discharge of firelocks by the friends who had just left us, thought we might have been attacked, and came out to our assistance.

We now resumed our march, and continued it till sunset, each boasting of his prowess, and what feats of arms he had before done, and what he would have done had the Bey's troops been hostile.

The evening we encamped in the open Desert, on a spot devoid of water, and so completely barren, that not even a single blade of herb for our camels was to be found, and we were obliged to feed them with what provender we had with us.

On the *second* day we advanced for twelve hours through the Desert, the plain consisting of soft limestone, sometimes bare, but more frequently covered with quicksand.

On the morning of the *third day*, the scene somewhat altered; detached hills rose here and there, taking from the uniformity of the before level desert. These mounds seemed to derive their origin from a base of calcareous rock, round, and on which the sands had gathered, and been heaped up by the winds, and on some to a considerable height. From this district of hillocks and hills, commences a range of mountains called *Morai-je*, stretching far to SSW, and seemingly also branching towards the north. This day we encamped two hours before sunset, for the purpose of awaiting the return of some *Twaters*, who separated from us about noon, to seek pasture for their camels. Our camp was pitched on the summit of a hill, at foot of which were spread a quantity of petrified shells and marine substances imbedded in a soft limestone.

On the *fourth day* we struck our tents very early in the morning, with the view of reaching a particular spot for our next encampment, where fresh water was to be found. The first part of our day's journey we travelled on a continued plain on the heights of the mountain. The ascent from the east had been gentle, but coming to the western declivity, we found the way down most steep and difficult. It is noted by the name of *Neddeek* by the Arabs. The way down is not only steep, but so narrow that the whole caravan was obliged to travel in single file, camel after camel. The perpendicular height of this (almost) precipice was about eighty feet. From the verge of the summit the prospect was most beautiful. A narrow vale, extending far beyond the reach of the eye, was illumined at some distance by the rise of sun, whose beams slanted over the mountain we had to pass : in regarding the level and brightness of the distant scene, we looked over a fore-ground of craggy rocks, and abrupt and frightful chasms yet remaining in gloomy shade ; and the contrast of bright and terrific scene made the stronger impression on our minds, whilst from this awful height we had to meditate on the difficulty and danger of our passage down to the plain. I followed not the narrow track of the caravan, but picked myself out a way down the mountain with some difficulty and risk. Coming to its base, I observed a piece of petrified wood, of about two feet long and eight inches broad; it was the only such fragment I saw in these parts. Forward in the plain to some distance, lay huge stones, or rather rocks. They probably have been there from the time of some great flood,* which, on every consideration of what I now and before saw, I must suppose to have inundated these countries, at some distant period, distinctively and subsequent to the deluge mentioned in Scripture. At some distance I cast a look back to the *Neddeek;* its appearance of wild forms of rock broken into or rent asunder, confirmed my idea of irruption of waters, and that the deluge had rushed from the west. Our march was now directed along the valley, skirted by mountains nearly of the same height and form as those we had passed; at length it expanded into a wider plain called *Sultin,* where, at one o'clock, and after ten hours journey we encamped, and with water in plenty to replenish our bags for the ensuing days.

The *fifth* and *sixth* days we journied on through this Desert; for so, from its barrenness and appearance, it may be justly termed, though throughout abounding in springs. The waters I should, however, suppose to be bitter, as the Arabs dig no wells in this district.

The *seventh* day our way lay between ranges of hills, and in the evening we came to a spot affording not only verdure but *trees,* and that to a considerable extent of country: under these trees we encamped, and continued travelling through a very grove the best part of the ensuing day, when our road opened to a desert chequered with hills, and scabeous calcareous rocks. From one of these eminences I first observed the mountainous region *Harutsch,* so known

* Vide Strabo, p. 49, 50; edit. Casaub.

to and dreaded by travellers. The marvellous narratives of calamity
therein suffered, and which had been recited to me on our way; and
the black and dreary appearances which the face of the country
offered to my view, roused my curiosity, and I pressed on before
the caravan to examine a lower mountain, which, like a promon-
tory jutted towards us before the rest. The soil of the desert near
was stony, the stones consisting of calcareous limestone. The
mountain presented the form of an imperfect cone: its strata I take
to have lain originally horizontal, as those of the hills passed on our
route, but from some convulsion, they are now broken, turned over,
and promiscuously confused. The substance of which the mountain
consists, on fracture, and as to colour, resembles the ferruginous
basalt; and such I take it to be. Range upon range of dreary and
black mountains succeed, and form the only prospect!

As the caravan was approaching, I dismounted, and sat me down
close to a large stone which formed my table, whilst I partook of
such frugal fare as the Arab carries with him on these occasions.
When I rose up the caravan had passed the prominence of the mountain and disappeared. The ground, however, being firm, and thence
the road to be easily traced, I was under no anxiety; though after
half an hour's march, somewhat surprised at not yet discovering my
old companions, I took out my spy-glass, when I descried at a little
distance four *Moroccans*, whom I rode up to and accosted: they told
me that the caravan had already encamped at a short distance from
the road, to pasture their camels, and that they themselves were in
search of water to satisfy their thirst. I was inclined to be of their
party, but was fearful of giving uneasiness to my people by longer
absence from the caravan, which, from its fires now kindled, I easily
discovered and rejoined.

The *ninth* day we travelled between black and dreary hills; our road meandering through narrow and dismal ravines, now and then spreading to some width, having some grass and even a tree, and sometimes opening to a space of valley, of which the herbage looked fresh, and even luxuriant, from the copious rains which fall in this mountainous region, fertilizing the soil after it is washed down.

Our watering-place consisted of pools of mere rain water from the hills, and was situate at the edge of a valley of about six miles circuit, shewing not only a rich verdure, but bearing shrubs and trees. Here we saw some *gazelles*, but so shy, that we could not get a shot at them.

We passed our *tenth, eleventh,* and *twelfth* days incessantly almost in march through this dreary solitude; yet we could not expedite our journey as we wished. Sometimes we were obliged to wander from our direct line with the windings of our only path; at other times we were forced to move on slowly and with difficulty, over layers of loose stone for half a mile together: in the course of one of those days, I ventured on a walk to the *south*, accompanied by my Arabian servant and some *Twaters*. We could easily, on foot, outstrip the caravan under all its impediments of march. Every where I found the mountains of like appearance as exhibited to the traveller on the common road, with the only difference that views even more dreary and terrific occasionally caught the eye : it having been matter of course to work and conduct the road along the least rugged vallies.

On the afternoon of the *thirteenth* day, we broke at length from

this dark region into an extensive plain. Here we continued on
march for some hours, when we came to ranges of low calcareous
mountains, and about sunset encamped at the entrance of the defile
which leads through them.

On the morning of the *fifteenth* I placed myself among the fore-
most of the caravan, consisting chiefly of poor pilgrims, hastening
to precede the other company, with a view of first quenching their
thirst at the spring, which on that day we were to arrive at. On
coming to the watering-place I perceived a *well* already cleaned
and in order, and several *Twaters* lying round. I placed myself
near and prepared for breakfast. An old man had laboured a
shorter cut across the sand to be sooner at the well ; after mutual
salutation, I offered him a handful of dates and some meat ; these
he thankfully accepted, kissing them and rubbing them on his
forehead. Putting the provisions down on the ground, he got to
the spring, and continued drinking for a considerable time, and
recited his prayer *Elham-Dulillah* with great devotion. He told
me, that for three days past he had been without his requisite portion of water. This man (as himself told me), was above sixty
years old ; and this was his third voyage from *Fez* to *Mecca*, without possessing the least means of accommodation for the journey ;
without preparation of food for his subsistence ; nay, even without
water, excepting what commiseration and the esteem in which his
pilgrimage was held, might procure for him, from the charity and
regard of travellers better provided in the caravan.

We reposed the rest of the day on this spot, distant from our
last encampment four hours march, and our chief dispatched a messenger to Mourzouk, to give notice of arrival of the caravan on the

frontier of the kingdom, and to bear a letter of respect to the sultan from each merchant individually.

And now, on the *sixteenth*, (dating by our departure from *Augila*), we came again to the society of men : a march of nine hours bringing us to *Temissa*, situated within the territory of Fezzan.

## SECTION II.

### *Observations on the Region of the Harutsch.*

THE mountainous desert of *Harutsch* is the most remarkable region that came within scope of my observation during this journey; its extent has been stated to me at seven days journey over, from north to south; and at five days from east to west: but in a subsequent voyage from Fezzan to Tripoly, I fell in again with a branch or tract of the *Harutsch*, and was there told, that it yet extended further to the *west*. At Mourzouk, too, I was informed of black mountains on the road leading southward to Bornou, on whose heights the climate was of very cold temperature, and whence the people of Mourzouk obtained their iron; and I conjecture that such mountainous tract may be a further branch of the *Harutsch*, though having indeed no positive information or proof of the immediate junction or connection of these regions.

The rugged, broken, and altogether wild and terrific scene which this desert tract affords, leads strongly to the supposition that its surface at some period took its present convulsed form and appearance from volcanic revolution. Its inequalities of ground are no where of great altitude. The general face of country shews continued ranges of hills, running in various directions, rising from eight to twelve feet only above the level of the intermediate ground; and between which branches, (on perfect flats, and without any gradual ascent of base or fore-ground,) rise up lofty insulated mountains, whose sides are exceeding steep from the very base. A mountain of this description, situated midway on journey over this desert, and north of our caravan road, is by the Arabs termed *Stres*; it has the appearance of being split from the top down to the middle. I was prevented from particular examination of it, but soon, on our caravan halting, had the opportunity of inspecting another of the same kind.

This mountain I perceived, from the foot to the summit, to be covered with detached stones, such as wholly constitute the lower hills. The small plain from which this mountain rose, was encompassed by rows of hills, such as above described, closely running into each other, and connected as a wall. The flat within was overspread with white quicksand, on which lay, irregularly scattered, large blocks of stone, of like nature and substance as that generally throughout this desert. With some trouble I procured a sample of the earthy stratum beneath the sand : it seemed to me, at the time, to have the appearance of ashes thrown out from a volcano ; but I have since lost the paper which contained the specimen, and cannot further confirm the accuracy of my first observation. In the vicinity of this mountain, I found stones of smaller bulk and a reddish colour, resembling that of burnt bricks ; some of these were one-half red, the other blackish ; the red part had not the same weight or density, on fracture, as the black : the former is more porous and spongy, and bears a general resemblance to slags or scoriæ.

The stony substance, of which the mass of these mountains consists, varies in colour and density ; in some parts heavy and compact, in others having small holes and cavities. These species of stone are intermingled, and I could not discover in either, any extraneous matter or substance.

The stratification or lay of these stones is perfectly horizontal, but often disturbed; parts of the first layer sinking into and mixing with the second below, and the second with the third. Sometimes the strata take an oblique direction; sometimes are promiscuously confused, and sometimes no strata appear at all; and a series of low hills is formed of one solid mass of rock, with fissures in direction to the north. The plain too shews occasionally level rock of the like nature and substance, in parts where bare of sand or soil. The whole of this region of hillocks, hills, rocks, and mountains, is, in parts, intersected by vales, occasionally having water; and though the soil is of white sand, yet it is so far fertile as to produce single trees, and pasturage for beasts; in these productive spots are frequently to be seen the tracks and slots of game. Often, when I thought I could so do without danger of losing my way, I struck into one of the narrow vales running apparently in the same direction as our caravan road; and occasionally led away to defiles becoming more narrow and rugged, I repented my indiscretion, whilst thus separated from my company, and exposed to attack from Bedouins, with dependence for safety on my single sabre and pistols. On regaining the caravan, it yet occurred that my danger had not been great, for what Arab robber could look for a traveller in such a tract, or suppose any hardy enough to wander therein from his troop, excepting, indeed, some wretched Moroccan pilgrim in search of water!

In the course of these excursions, on the side of one of these narrow vales, winding among the mountains, I observed a narrow branch or inlet, towards the termination of which the rocky heights from each side closed, and formed a cavern of about nine feet deep, and five feet wide; and, considering its appearance and situation in this desolate, obscure, and mournful region, I was inspired with feelings, as on viewing the entrance to the subterraneous world, and very passage, *ad inferos.*

My interpreter told me, that at some time when I had taken another path, and when the caravan was travelling about midway through the mountains, he saw a cavern in which the stones to a considerable depth were black, and that under these lay a stratum of white stones. On travelling afterwards from Fezzan to Tripoly, in continuation of the Harutsch, (as I supposed it), I myself observed ranges of basaltic hills, alternate with ranges of calcareous hills. My interpreter brought me a specimen of the white stone taken from the cave himself had seen, but I think was not happy in its selection, it consisting of a mere lump of indurated argillaceous earth, such as often adheres to limestone.

In respect to the many hills, and their curious ranges and direction, the *Harutsch* exhibits a similitude to the excrescences on the bordering mountains I refer to in a subsequent journey; it agrees too in the circumstance of single stones scattered on the surface, which, in the Harutsch, are distinguished as being only of one species or substance, peculiar to the district. There is too a further analogy in the plains formed of bare rock; and in the white quicksand covering other levels, and laying round the mountains, and up their base, though to no considerable height.

Contiguous to the *Harutsch-el-assuat,* or black Harutsch, lies the white Harutsch, or *Harutsch-el-abiat.* The country denoted by this appellation is a vast plain, interspersed with mounds or isolated hills, and spreads to the mountains rising towards Fezzan. The stones covering the surface of this plain have the appearance of being glazed, and so too every other substance, and even the rocks

which occasionally rise or project from the level.  Among the stones
are found fragments of large petrified marine animals, but mostly
shells closed up and insolidated.  These shells struck or thrown
forcibly on others, give a shrill sound, and the fracture presents a
vitreous appearance.

The low, bare, calcareous hills which border the plain, are, by
the Arabs, comprised in the *Harutsch-el-abiat;* but they are of a
nature very different.  Of all that I have seen, this range of hills
contains the most petrifactions.  These mountains rise immediately
steep from the level, and the matter of which they are formed is
alone friable limestone, in which the petrifactions are so loosely imbedded, that they may be taken out with ease; they consist of petrified conchs, snail-shells, fish, and other marine substances.  I found
heads of fish that would be a full burthen for one man to carry.  In
the adjacent vallies are shells in great number, and of the same kind
as those found on the great plain, and which, as I before mentioned,
have the appearance of being glazed.

## SECTION III.

*Arrival at Temissa, and further Journey.*

WE were yet an hour's march distant from Temissa, when the inhabitants of that place greeted the caravan with welcome and congratulation on arrival. They put questions without number, concerning our health, intermingling wishes for peace in the Arabian stile and manner. The incessant repetition of the same words appeared to me extraordinary, but I was soon given to understand, that it denoted polite manners, according to usage of the country. The more noble and educated the man, the oftener did he repeat his questions. A well dressed young man attracted my particular attention, as an adept in the perseverance and redundancy of salutation. Accosting an Arab of Augila, he gave him his hand, and detained him a considerable time with his civilities, when the Arab being obliged to advance with greater speed to come up again with his companions, the youth of Fezzan thought he should appear deficient in good manners if he quitted him so soon : for near half a mile he kept running by his horse, whilst all his conversation was, How dost thou fare? Well, how art thou thyself? Praised be God thou art arrived in peace! God grant thee peace! How dost thou do, &c. &c.

On our approach to Temissa, the pilgrims arranged themselves with their kettle drum and green flag. The merchants formed a troop, at head of the caravan, and pranced and curvetted their horses as they led on, and in this manner we passed on to our place of encampment near the town, whilst the women assembled without the walls, welcomed us in their Arabian custom with reiterated and joyful exclamation, to which we answered by discharge of our fire-arms; and these compliments continued till we pitched our tents in a grove of date trees.

All was gladness and felicitation this day throughout the caravan, and especially amongst the merchants. Perhaps for years past the caravan had not left Cairo with so gloomy and fearful a prospect as on the present occasion, when an army of Infidels had so suddenly assailed and taken the principal city of Africa, destroyed the ruling power of the Mamelukes, and threatened immediate abolition to the trade for slaves, on which the caravan principally subsists. It was but a few days after our leaving Cairo, that the appearance of an horde of Bedouins gave alarm to our caravan; indeed it was extraordinary that we should reach Siwah without attack, as the Arabs had of late been so bold, as even to pass the French posts, and rob near to the very capital. Whilst at Siwah, we were apprised of the movements of different hordes of Bengasi and other Arabian tribes; and not far from our road between Augila and the frontiers of Fezzan, we descried numerous vestiges of their depredation, viewing some hundreds of dead camels and beasts of burthen which they had plundered and left, probably from deficiency of water for their support. They had robbed in the neighbourhood, and even made an attack on Temissa, and had waited for us in these parts for a considerable time, till they concluded that, from the conquest of Cairo, our caravan would not this year proceed. Being therefore now in no immediate danger, and our future route laying through the inhabited districts of the realm of Fezzan, our fears at once vanished.

Temissa is at present a place of little importance, containing not more than forty men bearing arms. It is built on a hill, and surrounded by a high wall, capable of securing it against hostile incursion if in due repair, but in many parts the wall is decayed and fallen. I was told there were inscriptions to be discovered on some of the buildings, but I found none, and rather suppose none such ever existed, the ruins consisting of mere dilapidated houses, built with limestone, and cemented with a reddish mortar. These remains, however, shew that the ancient inhabitants of Temissa were more expert in the art of building than the present, who have patched up dwelling places in and among the ruins scarcely so comfortable as our sheds for cattle in Europe.

These people have many sheep and goats. Their only beast of burden is the ass. The place is surrounded with groves of date trees, which furnish the chief subsistence; corn is produced, but in very small quantity.

Having visited the town; on my return to camp, I found there a number of the natives, bartering sheep, fowls and dates, for tobacco, butter, female ornaments, and the coarse woollen stuffs with which the Arabs are generally cloathed. The evening closed in mutual congratulation and festivity, and the younger slaves and boys of the camp made a bonfire.

Our journies from this place being intended to be short, we did not decamp the following morning till half an hour after sunrise, and moved on slowly between date trees, on a generally level ground, interspersed here and there with low hills formed by the wind, which had gathered and heaped a deep sand round some of the trees, so that only the top branches appeared. At two in the afternoon, we came in sight of *Zuila*, and proceeded towards the place destined for our encampment SW. of the town.

## SECTION IV.

### Of Zuila.

ZUILA being a place of importance in the territory of Fezzan, and the place of residence, not only of many leading and wealthy men, but of relations to the family of the Sultan; we halted at some little distance from the town, and prepared to do the proper honours of our arrival.

The merchants, their pages and slaves dressed themselves in their best apparel; and the *Sheik* ordered his green flag to be borne before him, in honor to the *Shereefs* who live in this place. We had scarcely formed ourselves in procession, when we perceived twenty horsemen, mounted on white horses, with a green flag carried in their centre. It was the Shereef *Hindy*, the principal man of the town, who with his eight sons and other relations, was come out to meet us: at some distance followed a great number of men and boys on foot. They joined our caravan, and we passed together near the town, with huzzas and discharge of muskets, till we reached our place of encampment and pitched our tents.

Many other inhabitants then came out to us, some from curiosity and some to barter their goods; all behaved with the greatest decorum and regularity; but the family of the *Shereef* was distinguished by its particular complacency and politeness of manners: they wore the Tripolitan dress, but over it a fine Soudan shirt or *Tob*. The dealings of the caravan, on this occasion, were considerable, and especially with the women, who purchased various articles of ornament, in exchange for garden-stuff, milk, and poultry.

*Zuila* has received the name of *Belled-el-Shereef*, or town of the Shereefs: in former times it was an important place, and its circumference appears to have been thrice the extent of what it is now. Some of the Shereef's family told me, that some centuries past Zuila had been the residence of the sultans, and the general rendezvous of the caravans: and even yet the voyage to Fezzan is termed, the voyage to *Seela*, by the caravan from Bornou.

This little city stands on a space of about one mile in circuit; as in *Augila*, the houses have only a ground floor, and the rooms are lighted from the door. Near the centre of the town, are the ruins of a building several stories high, and of which the walls are very thick; and report says, this was formerly the palace. Without the town near the southern wall, stands an old mosque, little destroyed by time, serving as a sample of the ancient magnificence of Zuila; it contains in the middle a spacious hall or saloon, encompassed by a lofty colonnade, behind which runs a broad passage, with entrances to various apartments belonging to the establishment of the mosque. At some little distance further from the city, appear ancient and very lofty edifices, which are the tombs of shereefs, who fell in battle, at time the country was attacked by Infidels.

The environs of Zuila are level, supplied with water, and fertile. The groves of date trees are of great extent; and its inhabitants appear to pay more attention to agriculture than those of adjoining places.

In the evening we had further proof of the Arab hospitality of yore. A slave of the Shereef's, brought to each tent a dish of meat and broth, and ten small loaves; this most ancient custom the Sheik of the Sultan keeps up and strictly adheres to on arrival of each caravan; soon after, he sent to each of us three small loaves for the morrow's breakfast.

## SECTION V.

*Further journey—and arrival at Mourzouk.*

W E left the hospitable *Zuila* the ensuing morning, and having passed through a grove of date trees, came to an extensive and open plain over which we marched seven hours, and then arrived at *Hemara*; a small village, thin in people, and wretched in appearance, though the country round is most fertile. Here for the first time I was regaled with the great Fezzan dainty of locusts or grasshoppers, and a drink called *lugibi*. The latter is composed of the juice of date trees, and when fresh is sweet and agreeable enough to the taste, but is apt to produce flatulencies and diarrhœa. At first I did not relish the dried locusts, but when accustomed, grew fond of them: when eaten, the legs and wings are broken off and the inner part is scooped out, and what remains has a flavour similar to that of red herrings, but more delicious.

The succeeding day we were on march before sunrise; our road crossed a plain, with date trees to the south, among which I descried several small villages. I was till noon separated from my usual party, the Sultan's Sheik of Zuila being pleased to select me as his particular companion. His ordinary clothes were very much worn, and even ragged; he had a cloak, the badge of his high office; he chose to ride with me (as he said) because he deemed it dishonour to ride with the merchants. When permitted to quit him and rejoin my old comrades, I found them in great glee and spirits, at being so near the place where they had houses and families;

their gladness, however, soon received alloy, for the officers of the Sultan met us to take account of the bales and merchandize, which had not being usually done till arrival at the gates of Mourzouk; and the merchants had been in the habit of previously disposing of at least a third of their goods, in order to evade the duties. Some however, had contrived to intermingle their baggage with that of the pilgrims, who pay no duties. Rather out of humour with what had passed, our traders of the caravan agreed with a proposal of the Sheik to make a forced march to *Tragen,* where we arrived at sunset.

At this place we reposed the whole of the ensuing day, employed in preparation for honourable appearance before the Sultan, who usually rides out to meet the caravan, in pious respect to the pilgrims returning from Mecca. The Sultan sent forward some camels laden with meat and bread, which were here distributed. The next morning we proceeded, and after eight hours march, pitched our camp near to the chapel and tomb of *Sidibischir,* a holy man of great renown in ancient times, and from whom the village near is likewise named *Sidibischir.* The following day was to be that of our interview with the Sultan. On that day, the 17*th of November,* we finished our long and perilous journey, arriving, after a three hours march, in the immediate vicinities of Mourzouk.

The Sultan had posted himself on a rising ground, attended by a numerous court, and a multitude of his subjects.

Our caravan halted, and every person of the caravan, of any importance, dismounted to salute him. With others I approached, and found the sultan seated on an old-fashioned elbow chair, covered with a cloth striped red and green, and placed at extremity of an oval area, round which soldiers were drawn up, of but mean appearance. The sultan himself wore the Tripolitan vest, and over it a shirt or frock, embroidered with silver, in the Soudan manner. Close to him, on each side, were white Mamelukes and Negro slaves, with drawn sabres; behind these were six banners, and black and half-naked slaves, holding lances and halberds, of a fashion as old perhaps, as the times of Saladin. We entered the circle by an opening left facing the sultan, and about the middle of the area: according to the ceremonial of his court, we pulled off our slippers, and approached barefoot to kiss his imperial hand. Each having paid his compliment, alternately passed to right or left, and seated himself behind the sultan : the merchants being thus ranged in two equal groups on either side the throne; lastly entered the Sheik of the pilgrims, with his sabre drawn, and kettle-drum, and green flag of Mecca borne before him. The pilgrims followed, chaunting praises to God, who had so far conducted them in safety; and continued their hymns until the Sultan was pleased to dismiss their leader, with a gracious promise of sending his royal present of dates and meat to every tent. This ceremony of audience being over, the Sultan remounted his horse and rode back to the city of Mourzouk, preceded by kettle-drums and banners, and amidst his lance-men and halberdiers; whilst his courtiers, joined by the Arabs of our caravan, pranced and curvetted their horses on each flank of the procession.

# CHAPTER III.

*Some Account of Fezzan.*

THE greatest length of the *cultivated part* of the kingdom of
Fezzan, is about 300 English miles from north to south, and the
greatest width 200 miles from east to west; but the mountainous
region of *Harutsch* to the east, and other deserts to the south and
west, are reckoned within its territory.

The borderers on the north are Arabs, nominally dependant on
Tripoly, but their obedience is merely nominal, and they take each
opportunity of public weakness or commotion to throw off the yoke.
Fezzan to the east is bounded by the *Harutsch*, and line of deserts.
To the south and south-east is the country of the Tibboes. To the
south-west that of the Nomadic Tuaricks. On the west are Arabs.

The kingdom contains a hundred and one towns and villages, of
which Mourzouk is the capital. The principal towns next in order
to the imperial residence are *Sockna, Sibha, Hun,* and *Wadon* to the
north; *Gatron* to the south; *Yerma* to the west; and *Zuila* to the
east.

The climate of Fezzan is at no season temperate or agreeable.
During the summer the heat is intense; and when the wind blows
from the south is scarcely supportable, even by the natives. The

winter might be moderate were it not for the prevalence of a bleak and penetrating north wind during that season of the year, and which chilled and drove to the fire not only the people of the place, but even myself, the native of a northern country.

It rains at Fezzan seldom, and then but little in quantity. From November 1798 to June 1799, there was not a single thunder storm; the 31st of January, 1799, there were some faint lightnings without thunder. Tempests of wind are however frequent, both from the north and the south, whirling up the sand and dust, so as to tinge the very atmosphere yellow. There is no river, nor indeed a rivulet deserving note throughout the whole country. The soil is a deep sand covering calcareous rock or earth, and sometimes a stratum of argillaceous substance.

Dates may be termed the natural and staple produce of Fezzan. In the western parts of the kingdom some senna is grown, and of a quality superior to that imported from the country of the Tibboes. Pot-herbs, and generally vegetables of the garden, are plentiful. Wheat and barley are suited to the soil and climate, but from inexpertness or difficulties attending the mode of tillage, and generally from indolence of the people and oppressions of the government, corn is not raised sufficient for the inhabitants, and they rely for subsistence on importations from the Arab countries bordering Fezzan to the north.

Very little attention is bestowed on the rearing of beasts. Horned cattle are to be found only in the most fertile districts; and are even there but few in number; they are employed in drawing water from the wells, and are slaughtered only in cases of extreme necessity. The ordinary domestic animal is the goat. Sheep are bred in the

southern parts of the kingdom ; but the general supply is furnished
by the bordering Arabs   The wool is manufactured into *abbes*, or
coarse woollen cloths, the general clothing throughout the country;
with the meat the very skins are roasted, whilst fresh, and eaten.
The horses are but few: asses are the beasts of general use, whether
for burthen, draught, or carriage. Camels are excessively dear, and
only kept by the chief people, or richer merchants. All these
animals are fed with dates or date kernels.

The commerce of Fezzan is considerable, but consists merely of
foreign merchandize. From October to February, Mourzouk is the
great market and place of resort for various caravans from Cairo,
Bengasi, Tripoly, Gadames, Twat, and Soudan, and for other
smaller troops of traders, such as Tibboes of Rschade, Tuaricks,
and Arabs. The trade from Cairo is carried on by the merchants
of *Augila*; that from Tripoly, chiefly by the inhabitants of *Sockna*,
and but by few either of Fezzan or Tripoly. The commerce with
Soudan, is conducted by way of the *Tuarick Kolluvi*, by the native
*Agades*; the trade with Bornou is managed by the *Tibboes* of *Bilma*. The caravans coming to Mourzouk from the south or west,
bring, as articles of commerce, slaves of both sexes, ostrich feathers,
zibette, tiger skins, and gold, partly in dust, partly in native grains,
to be manufactured into rings and other ornaments, for the people
of interior Africa. From *Bornou* copper is imported in great quantity. Cairo sends silks, *melayes* (striped blue and white calicoes),
woollen cloths, glass, imitations of coral, beads for bracelets, and
likewise an assortment of East India goods. The merchants of
*Bengasi*, who, usually join the caravan from Cairo at *Augila*, import
tobacco manufactured for chewing, or snuff, and sundry wares fabri-
cated in Turkey.

The caravan from Tripoly, chiefly deals in paper, false corals, fire-arms, sabres, knives, and the cloths called *abbes*, and in red worsted caps. Those trading from *Gadames*, bring nearly the same articles. The smaller caravans of *Tuaricks* and *Arabs*, import but-ter, oil, fat, and corn; and those coming from the more southern districts, bring senna, ostrich feathers, and camels for the slaughter-house.

Fezzan is governed by a sultan, descendant from the family of the Shereefs. The tradition is, that the ancestors of the reigning prince, coming from western Africa, invaded and conquered Fezzan about 500 years past. The sultan reigns over his dominions with unlimited power, but he holds them tributary to the Bashaw of Tripoly: the amount of tribute was formerly 6000 dollars, it is now reduced to 4000 ; and an officer of the bashaw comes annually to Mourzouk, to receive this sum, or its value in gold, senna, or slaves. This officer, whilst in commission, is called *Bey-el-nobe*. On his departure from Tripoly, which is every year in November, he takes all travelling merchants under his protection; and returning from Tripoly to Mourzouk, I shall avail myself of the opportunity.

The present sultan assumes the title " Sultan Muhammed-ben Sultan Mansur;" and this title is engraved on a large seal, which he applies to acts of authority or correspondence within his realm, but when writing to the bashaw of Tripoly, he uses a smaller seal, on which, instead of the name *Sultan*, that of *Sheik* only, is engraved.

The throne of Fezzan is hereditary : the crown, however, de-scends not in all cases, directly from father to son : it is the eldest prince of the royal family, who succeeds; and such may be a

nephew, in preference to a son who is younger. This custom frequently occasions bloodshed: the son of the deceased sultan may
be of sufficient age to govern, though younger than the collateral
heir; and having interest and adherents formed by his past high
connections and situation, will often be ready to controvert the law
of succession, as inapplicable in principle to the case of himself and
competitor, equally arrived at the age of manhood and discretion :
the question of right is then decided by the sword.

The Sultan's palace (or house) is situate within the circumvallation of the castle or fortress of Mourzouk : he lives there retired,
and with no other inmate but the eunuchs, who wait upon him.
His Harem is contiguous; he never enters it, but the female whom
he at any time wishes to see, is conducted to his apartment. The
Harem consists of a Sultana, who, by rules of the empire, must be
of the family of the Shereefs of *Wadan* or *Zuila*, and of about forty
slaves. These last are often sold and replaced by others, if they do
not bear children to the sultan, or do not otherwise endear themselves to him by superior charms and accomplishments.

There is a place set apart within the precincts of the castle, for
those who attend on public business, from which a long narrow
vestibule leads to a door which opens into the principal apartment of
the sultan. The opening of that door is announced by the beating
of kettle-drums, as a signal of audience. The door of audience is
opened three times in each day. Those who on account of respect
or business, attend for introduction, are conducted by the long
narrow passage between slaves, who incessantly repeat, " May God
prolong the life of the sultan !" On coming to the door, the sultan
appears opposite, seated on an old fashioned elbow chair raised some
steps, and forming his throne. The person introduced, approaches,

kisses the hand of the sultan, raises it so as to touch his forehead, then quits it, and kneels before him. He is permitted to state his case, and address the sultan in ordinary and plain language, but particular attention must be given, that the expressions, " God prolong thy life ;" " God protect thy country, &c." be frequently intermingled ; and at each presentation, it is customary to offer a small present. It is only on Fridays, or on some solemn festival, that the sultan appears without the castle walls, and then he is attended by his whole court. He goes on Fridays to the great mosque, on horseback : on other days of solemnity or public occasion, he rides on a plain without the town, where his courtiers prance and run their horses round him, and exhibit their skill in equestrian exercises, and in the art of shooting.

The sultan's court or official attendants are, the *kaledyma*, or first minister ; the *keijumma*, or second minister, and the general of his forces ; a number of black slaves, and a few white slaves, who are by the Mahometans termed Mamelukes. The *kaledyma* and *keijumma* must both be free-born men ; whatever their nominal rank, they at present have but little influence. All the interest and power rests with the Mamelukes, who are mostly Europeans, Greeks, Genoese, or their immediate descendants. The black slaves, are purchased whilst yet boys, and are educated for the court according to their dispositions and talents ; some of these too have gained great ascendancy with the sultan.

The apparel of the sultan, on days of state and ceremony, consists of a large white frock or shirt, made in the Soudan manner, of stuff, and brocaded with silver and gold, or of satin interwoven with silver. Under this frock, he wears the ordinary dress of the Tripolitans ; but the most remarkable appearance is that of his turban, which, from the fore to the hinder part, extends a full yard, and is not less than two thirds of a yard in breadth.

The revenues of the sultan are produced from certain assessments of tax on all gardens and cultivated lands, and from arbitrary fines and requisitions. The slaves employed in collecting these imposts, are most exorbitant and oppressive, if not bribed. The sultan derives further income from duties on foreign trade, paid by the several caravans. That from Cairo pays from six to eight dollars for each camel load. The caravans from Bornou and Soudan pay two *matkals*, for each slave on sale. He further possesses a territorial revenue, collected from domains of the crown ; from salt-pools ; from the natron lakes; and from the royal gardens and woods. The present sultan has made great addition to his treasures by predatory expeditions, which he occasionally directs against the *Tibboes* of the tribe of *Burgu*.

The public expenditure consists chiefly in maintenance of the sultan, his court, and palace. The cadi and department of justice, those of the religious order, and the great officers of government, are severally supported from the produce of date-tree woods and gardens, granted as *usufruct* to those holding the respective offices. The princes of the royal family are supported from the proceeds of appropriate territory, and by certain proportions of corn delivered weekly from the sultan's stores, and from occasional exactions on the people, levied by their personal authority, and by means of their slaves. Such oppression is a natural result of the powers of collection, and means of enforcement, and adjudication of right, being vested in each occasional lord of the domain.

Justice is administered by an officer, termed the cadi : his decisions are directed by the Mahometan law, old customs, and established practice; with exception to criminal cases, in which judgment is arbitrary, or referred to the sultan. In the absence of the cadi, his secretary or scribe, performs the office.

The dignity of a cadi, or chief judge, is hereditary in a certain family, ever since the present race of sultans was established on the throne. The sultan, in each instance of demise or vacancy, selects from this family, such individual to fill the office of cadi, as is noted for learning; or in other words, *who can best read and write.*

Besides the cadi, all the princes of the sultan's family, claim a right of jurisdiction, and even of imposing corporal punishments.

The cadi is, at the same time, chief of the clergy, and possesses great influence and authority with the people; the next to him in rank, is the *iman kbir*, or great Iman.

The population of Fezzan is not easily determined. On loose estimate, I should state the inhabitants throughout, at about 70, or 75,000 souls. All of them, without exception, profess the Mahometan religion. The colour or complexion of the people varies; those of the northern parts of the country, for the most part, have a complexion and features, similar to those of the Arabs. In the southern districts, they have mixed with the natives of the great nations bordering on that quarter, and bear a resemblance to the Tibboes and to the Tuaricks. The genuine or indigenous race of Fezzans, may be described as a people of but ordinary stature, and their limbs by no means muscular or strong, their colour a deep brown, their hair black and short, their form of face such as, in

Europe, we should term regular, and their nose less flattened than that of the negro.

The mein, the walk, and every motion and gesture of the people of Fezzan, denote a want of energy, either of mind or body. The tyrannic government, the general poverty of the country, and their only food consisting of dates, or a kind of farinaceous pap, with no meat, and rarely with even a little rancid oil or fat, contribute at once to weakness of frame, and dejection of spirit. Even in those parts, where the race may be supposed to be ameliorated by a mixture with the Arabs, there is no energy of character, no industry. Arts and manufactures, will of course supply but a poor and scanty chapter, exhibiting few articles, and no ingenuity : throughout Mourzouk, I could not find one single skilful artificer in any trade or work ; indeed, there are no other tradesmen, but shoemakers and smiths. The latter work every metal without distinction; and the same man who forges shoes for the sultan's horse, makes rings for his princesses. The women, indeed, fabricate coarse woollen cloths, called *abbes ;* but for the goodness or value of their manufacture the reader may form his own estimate, when told, that the weaver's shuttle is unknown, and that the woof is inserted into the warp thread by thread, and the whole worked solely by hand.

The dress of the people of Fezzan consists of a shirt or frock, made of a coarse linen or cotton cloth, brought from Cairo, and the *abbe* so often mentioned. The middling classes wear frocks made at Soudan, of dyed blue cloth. The richer people and the Mamelukes of the sultan are clothed in the Tripolitan habit, over which they wear a Soudan shirt of variegated pattern and colours, and likewise the *abbe.* The ornamental distinctions of dress are chiefly confined to the head-dress, and to rings on the arms and legs. The lady of a chief or wealthy man of Fezzan divides her hair into seven long curls or tresses; one of these is interbraided with long slips of gilt leather, terminating in a bow; the other six tresses are bound round by a gilt leather strop, and at the end of each is a trinket, which a sketch will best describe.

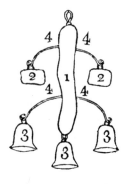

No. 1.     A long stick of coral.

2, 2.     Small pieces of amber.

3, 3, 3.  Little silver bells.

4, 4.     Silver or brass wire.

In addition to these ornaments, the Fezzan woman fastens to the top of her head silken cords, on which are strung a number of silver rings, and which hang on each side pendant to her shoulder. The ears of ladies of rank are bored in two places, and in each hole is fixed a thick silver ring. In ordinary dress they wear nine or ten rings of horn or glass on each arm, four or five of which are taken off on all great occasions, to make room for a silver armillary of four inches breadth. They wear at the same time strong rings of brass or silver just above the ankle bones. The necklace consists of a silk riband, to which are fixed ten or twelve pieces of agate, and in front a round silver plate. The meaner women wear merely a string of glass beads, and curl their hair above the forehead into large ringlets, into which severally is stuffed a paste made of lavender, carraway-seeds, cloves, pepper, mastick, and laurel leaves, mixed up with oil.

The women of Fezzan generally have a great fondness for dancing and every amusement, and the wanton manners and public freedoms which, although Mahometans, they are permitted, astonishes the Mahometan traveller.  They dance publicly in the open places of the town, not only in the day-time, but even after sunset.  Two or three men stand together with their tambourines; the women immediately form a circle round; the men beat a tune, and those in the circle accompany it with singing and clapping of hands; a girl then advances dancing towards the drummers; the men, as she approaches near, join in the dance and press towards her; on which she makes some steps backwards, and then falls on her back with her body and limbs stiff and perfectly straight, when the women behind catch her in the fall, a few spans from the ground, and toss her in the air, whence she descends on her feet.  The men then resume their station in the centre, and a second female dancer repeats the sport, which is successively engaged in by each brisk damsel of the circle.

The men of Fezzan are much addicted to drunkenness.  Their beverage is the fresh juice of the date tree, called *lugibi*, or a drink called *busa*, which is prepared from the dates, and is very intoxicating.  When friends assemble in the evening, the ordinary amusement is mere drinking; but sometimes a singing girl, or *kadanka*, is sent for: *kadanka* is a Soudan word, and answers to the term *almé* used at Cairo.

The song of these Fezzan girls is Soudanic.  Their musical instrument is called *rhababe*: it is an excavated hemisphere, made from a shell of the gourd kind, and covered with leather; to this a long handle is fixed, on which is stretched a string of horse hairs longitudinally closed and compact as one cord, about the thickness of a quill. This is played upon with a bow. I was once of a party with *Sidi Mintesser*, the brother of the sultan, at a small house, some distance from the palace, when he ordered a *Kadanka* to be brought, and with whom he soon after withdrew. On her return to the company, she was asked with a significant smile where she had been. She immediately took up her instrument, played upon it, and sung, in the Arabian language, " Sweet is Sidi Mintesser, as the waters of the Nile, but yet sweeter is he in his embraces; how could I resist?" As a natural consequence of the great freedoms allowed to the sex in Mourzouk, there are more women of a certain description to be found in that capital, than in any other of the same extent and population; and the general character of improvidence, and consequent misery and distress, belong as fully to the frail sisterhood of this place, as of any other.

There are various sorts of venereal disorders prevalent in Fezzan; that imported from Soudan is the worst. The common lues venerea brought from Tripoly and Cairo, is called *franzi*, or the *frank* evil. For the cure of either species they use salts, and the fruit *handal*, (colycinth), as powerful cathartics; and the sores, if any, are at the same time washed with natron water, or dissolved soda. These remedies seldom fail, unless the disease has taken a very deep root.

The other maladies prevalent here are hæmorrhoides, no doubt greatly increased by the immoderate use of red pepper; and a fever and ague, which is particularly dangerous to foreigners. In these disorders there is no remedy whatever known or used but amulets, consisting of certain sentences, transcribed from the Koran, on a slip of paper, which the patient wears about his neck, and in bad cases is made to swallow. Phlebotomy is unknown; but blood is occasionally drawn by means of cupping. As to surgery, I heard there were people at Mourzouk who had sufficient ability to cure a simple fracture.

The houses of the Fezzans are miserably built; they are constructed with stones or bricks made of a calcareous earth mixed with clay, and dried in the sun. No other tools are used in the building but the hands of the labourer. When the walls are completely raised, the friends of the proprietor assemble, and assist him to incrust and cover them with a mortar made with a white calcareous earth. This work too is done only by the hand. The houses are all extremely low, and the light enters by the door only.

As to diet, I never knew a more abstemious people than those of Fezzan. Meat indeed is a food they can at no time abstain from when set before them; but meat is not an article of food with the people in general: to indicate *a rich man*, at Mourzouk, the usual expression is, " *that he eats bread and meat every day.*"

### POSTSCRIPT.

THE particulars above communicated may give some general idea of Mourzouk, and of the people and kingdom of Fezzan. Proposing shortly to return into that country, I may have an opportunity of gaining more satisfactory intelligence, and of enlarging on some points, and of rectifying any mistake in others; I will then draw up for the Society a more full and amended account, having in view the means of conveyance through one of my country-friends, who is going with the caravan to Mourzouk, and proposes returning to Tripoly in May or June 1800, when he will consign my papers to the care of the British Consul.

(Signed)                    FREDERICK HORNEMAN.

# APPENDIX. No. I.

*Observations on F. Horneman's Description of the Country and Anti-*
*quities of Siwah, with Reference to ancient Accounts of the* Oasis,
*and* Temple of Ammon. *By Sir William Young, Bart. Secretary.*

T H E papers alluded to in Mr. Horneman's Postscript have never
been received; and nearly two years having elapsed since the date
from which our expectation was referred, the above more sum-
mary account of his Travels (as probably the only one extant)
is offered for perusal. Opportunities of correspondence from the
interior of Africa can rarely occur, but by the caravans passing
at certain, but distant, periods of time; and even by such conveyance, any communication from an European and Christian traveller, must be conducted with so particular a caution in avoidance
of offence to the bigotry and prejudices of the people, that Mr.
Horneman's intentions of again writing may not only have been
delayed, but wholly precluded, by the circumstances of his situation.
The necessity of sustaining the character of a Mussulman unconnected with those termed " the Infidels of Christendom," is strongly
impressed in his letters from Cairo, Aug. 31, 1798, wherein he ear-
nestly deprecates even inquiry concerning him, as liable to awaken
jealousies and suspicions in the natives who may be so questioned;
and any farther communications at present, from himself, may be
matter of similar apprehension.

Under these considerations, it is become a duty to his public-spi-
rited employers, that such curious intelligence as their traveller has
already given, should no longer be withheld, even in its present
state, and for which they will make a just and candid allowance.

It is however presumed, that the Reader will not have found in perusal of this Journal, that there is much which may require his favour or excuse : yet some details appear to need explanation, and which (if a reference to the traveller himself were possible) might be given in a manner the most clear and satisfactory.

In default of such advantage, the Editor offers an annotation or comment on two subjects of peculiar interest, treated of in this Journal, and in a manner apparently incorrect, or contradictory to accounts given by other writers.

Page 15; the extent of the Oasis of Siwah, (as represented by Mr. Horneman) differs widely from that stated by every other writer ancient or modern.

Page 23; the admeasurements of the sacred Egyptian building appear to vary in every proportion from those given by a late traveller of allowed accuracy, Mr. Brown.

In the first instance, it is the purpose of the Annotator to ascertain the error, and to shew whence it has arisen.

In the second case, he will have to place the subject in a point of view, by which an apparent variation in the two accounts may not only be reconciled, but even matter of new and just inference, as to the ancient construction and purpose of the building in question, be shewn to arise, from the very elucidation which corrects and compares these differences.

Page 15; Mr. Horneman states " *the principal and fertile territory of Siwah to be fifty miles in circuit :*" in this he disagrees with every account given by the writers cited by Mr. Rennell, and with that latterly given by Mr. Brown, who, in conformity with the descriptions by other authors, states the extent of the Oasis, or fertile spot, to be six miles in length, and four miles and a half in breadth; not exceeding eighteen miles in circumference at the utmost. It will further appear that, in this respect, Horneman is not only at variance with the writings of others, but with his own, and that his own journal furnishes the strongest internal evidence in refutation of the fact he asserts.

Horneman names all the towns within the territory of Siwah,— *Scharkie*, *Msellem*, *Monachie*, *Sbocka*, and *Barischa*, and he places all these villages, or towns, within *one or two miles* of Siwah the capital, which proximity could not be the case, if the rich and fertile land extended each way sixteen miles in traverse, as a circle of fifty miles implies. On a small and most fertile tract of country, surrounded on all sides by barren and sandy deserts, the rich and productive soil infers a population commensurate with, and in proportion to, its extent. Diodorus Siculus tells us, that the ancient Ammonians dwelt κωμηδὸν, *i. e.* vicatìm. ( Ed. Wesseling, Tom. II. p. 198.) And so too the people at present (on grounds probably of convenience and defence against the Arabs of the Desert) appear to live chiefly in towns; and hence those towns must have been more distant, as more widely diffused over so great a space of country from its very character and description, to be supposed in every part occupied and appropriate. Society must have gathered and increased till it fully covered a country of such *exclusive* fertility and means of subsistence. Generally, increase of population is to be measured by the means of subsistence; and in converse of the proposition, whatever of country was productive and habitable situated as the Oasis of Siwah, must be considered as inhabited and

turned to account : the general reasoning and estimate of increase
of people is further strengthened by the special argument of probable resort, from the barren yet partially inhabited districts which
encompassed it.

Horneman's description of the territory of Siwah tallies with,
and confirms, the speculation : he represents the country as consisting of so many gardens walled or fenced on every side, and cultivated with so nice attention and labour, and with such care in
irrigation, that the water directed in various cuts and channels from
each spring, was in no case suffered to flow beyond the territory;
but was made to lose and expend itself in the cultivated grounds of
the Siwahans : and he describes the people as a swarm, and their
residence as a crowded hive.

Let us now advert to his more particular enumeration of these
Siwahans, and to the practicability of such number (as under any
computation can be supposed labourers in the field) being compe-
tent to work the ground of fifty miles in circuit, with the nice agriculture he describes.

Horneman states 1500 warriors, or *men bearing arms*, as the *data*
for estimating the population of the country : he must mean to
say, *men capable of bearing arms*, or there are no *data*, and he
means nothing. Calculate a population on the widest latitude from
such data, and apply it to a well-cultivated district of 127,360 square
acres, and there will not be more than one cultivator to at least
50 cultivated acres : for the women, our journalist has otherwise
engaged. They (as he tells us,) are employed in manufacture, and
chiefly in that of wicker-work and baskets, which they work with
great neatness and ingenuity. These statements carry self-con-

tradiction. These lands cannot be so extensive, or cannot be so cultivated.

Thus from Mr. Horneman's own account, we may infer, that the rich spot of country termed the Oasis of Siwah, must be of much less extent indeed, than that which he directly states.

Observing particular expressions in the Journal relative to this subject, the cause of error may possibly appear. The traveller says, " the territory of Siwah is of considerable extent ; its principal and most fertile district is a well watered valley of about fifty miles in circuit, *bemmed in by steep and barren rocks."*

Now, referring to other descriptions of the fertile district or Oasis of Siwah, it is to be remarked, that such rich and productive spot of country is no where described, as *immediately* bounded and hemmed in by steep rocks and mountains. Diodorus, lib. xvii. speaking of the Oasis of Ammon, says, it was surrounded on all sides by barren and arid sands : so too, Mr. Brown mentions the fertile soil or Oasis, of from four miles and an half in breadth, to six in length, as bordered and encompassed by " *desert land ;"* intimating *plain.* In truth, it is such desert border of plain, which further on is bounded by rocky mountains. Mr. Horneman appears to have made no excursions from the town of Siwah, further than *of a mile and a half* to the ruins, and *of one mile* to the catacombs of *El-Mota.* From all these considerations, it may be surmised, that our travel- ler looking from Siwah, or its adjacencies, to the hills or rocks surrounding him at a distance, comprized in his estimate of rich country, the whole intermediate plain, not having directed due in- quiry or consideration in the ascertaining of, to what extent within the area of that plain, the rich and cultivated soil might reach ? Or, perhaps, he *did* make enquiries; but of some patriotic Siwahan, who thought proper to exaggerate the richness and extent of his petty commonwealth, and confirm his hyperbole, by pointing to the lofty boundary in view : or, perhaps, from not sufficiently understanding the dialect of Siwah, (as the traveller himself allows,) he may have confounded the ideas of *country occupied*, and of *territory claimed.*

Be these surmises and explanations founded or not, our journalist's representation of the extent of the Oasis of Siwah, is not only at variance with every other account, but with the internal evidence to be extracted from his own account, and must be rejected as erroneous.

Page 23, of the Journal, to which this note refers, a further subject of inquiry and explanation occurs, where Mr. Horneman, describing the ruins of an ancient edifice in the vicinity of Siwah, gives us dimensions and proportions, in every respect differing from those before stated by Mr. Brown, in description of the same building.

|                           | The length in feet. | The width. | The height. |
|---------------------------|---------------------|------------|-------------|
| By Mr. Brown, -     -     | 32                  | 15         | 18          |
| By Mr. Horneman, 30 to 36 |                     | 24         | 27          |

Mr. Horneman informs us, that he was successively interrupted on entrance into the area of these ruins, and was altogether prevented by the jealousy of the natives, from pursuing any plan of accurate examination or admeasurement. The dimensions which he gives us, are therefore to be taken as the result of computation on mere view; and from these and other circumstances, it is further to be presumed, that such computation by view, was made *from without;* whilst Mr. Brown expressly tells us, that he took his measurements *in the clear*, or *inside* of the building.

In this case, a deduction equal to the thickness of the walls, is to be made from the length and the breadth of the building, as described by Mr. Horneman.

The thickness of the *end* walls may be supposed to be much less than that of the *side* walls, which being constructed to support the vast and ponderous blocks of stone which formed the roof, must have been built with a proportionate strength and solidity, not necessary, and probably therefore not used, at the entrance or end of the building. Mr. Horneman, indeed, when stating the thickness of the walls to be *six feet*, makes no such discrimination; but it may be fairly presumed, that adverting particularly (as he does,) to the massive roof, he meant to note exclusively, the strength of that part of the fabric by which it was supported.

Under such probable conjecture, the length and breadth of the building given by Mr. Brown *from the inside*, and by Mr. Horneman *from the outside*, may so far agree, as fully to exculpate our Journalist from any charge of inattention in his survey, or inaccuracy in his representations; making those allowances which his situation and circumstances, and (above all,) his own declarations of want of precision, fully intitle him to.

The comparative height of the building is a part of the subject, which suggests matter of new and interesting investigation.

Page 23, Mr. Horneman informs us, " *that the northern part of the building is erected on a native calcareous rock, rising about eight feet above the level of the area, within a circumvallation,*" which he particularly and exclusively describes, and which will be a subject of further dissertation. He then mentions, " that two vast stones of the roof have fallen in from the southern part of the building, and lay with their bottom nearly on a level with the plain of the outward enclosure;" and he was thence led to conjecture, that the base or floor of the southern division, was originally lower than that of the northern end.

The difference in measurement or estimate of height stated by the two travellers, strongly corroborates the fact.

It may be premised, that when an object is of no great altitude, an estimate of height may be made on mere inspection or view, with much more accuracy than any other line of dimension. A comparison with known objects, the stature of any human figure near, nay, the very person of the observer himself, will furnish a sort of scale for reference, by which he may compute from four to five times his own height with considerable precision.

A difference so great as that of from eighteen to twenty-seven feet in estimating the altitude of the building at Siwah, could not occur between two the most hasty and inaccurate observers, in noting the height of the same object. The object itself, therefore, must be considered as different; and in the one case, to be that of the *wall within*, and in the other case, that of *the temple from without.*

Mr. Brown taking his measurements in the clear, would ascertain the perpendicular of the wall from a part of the pediment or floor, the most clear and perfect; and this was, at the northern end. The dilapidations in the southern part of the building, do not appear to have attracted his notice in any other consideration, than as mere ruins: and merely as such, the unequal and broken surface would not be preferred for placing a rod in measurement to the summit, or from whence to look up and make a calculation of height. Mr. Brown accordingly measured the height from a proper base at the northern end, and found it to be eighteen feet. It has been already cited from the journal of Mr. Horneman, that the northern end was built on an isolated rock, rising eight feet above the plain of the general enclosure. The top of the wall from north to south, must have run on a level, and in a direct line : and the actual building of the southern part must have been eight feet higher than that of the northern end; and the entire building *from without* must have appeared, and in truth, have been, twenty-six feet high, even to conform with Mr. Brown's description from within.

The two travellers in other points agree, as to the architecture of the building, and sculpture on the walls, concurring in proof, that it was of the highest antiquity, and of Egyptian origin.

The division of the edifice exclusively noticed by Mr. Horneman, may give some further indication of its use and purpose, and per- haps may be found to strengthen the conjecture, " that these are the very ruins of the once famous oracular temple consecrated by the *Egyptian* Danaus, to the divinity of Ammon."

The writer of this note will on no account, and in no degree, dis- cuss the position of country, within which the renowned temple of Ammon was erected. He considers that question as concluded, and for ever set at rest, in the acute and learned comment on the Geo- graphy of Herodotus, by Mr. Rennell. The facts, the arguments, and the inferences stated in that admirable work, indisputably shew the Oasis of Siwah, to have been the Oasis of Ammon. The pre- cincts are thus narrowed, within which our researches are to be directed, for ascersaining the locality, and even the very remains of the temple itself: and this concurrent circumstance will be held in mind, whilst certain details in the description given us of the ruins discovered at Siwah, are examined and brought to the test, by reference to such few particulars as are recorded by ancient writers concerning the temple of Ammon.

The general description of the materials, of the architecture, and of the sculptures, may render it unnecessary to prolong this essay, by discussing the question of *when*, and *by whom* was the building erected? Those who may yet entertain a doubt, that it was a most ancient Egyptian edifice, are referred to the writings of Norden, of Pocock, of Lucas, and above all, to the treatise of Major Rennell above cited. The annotator ventures to assume the fact; and merely add, τὸ μὲν τέμενος φασὶν ἱδρύσασθαι Δαναὸν τον Αιγύπ]ιον. Diod. Sic. Tom. II. Ed. Wesseling. page 198.

So much as to the building and its antiquity being taken for granted; the following comment will advert to circumstances exclusively noticed by Mr. Horneman, and which may lead to further inferences, as to its original purpose and designation.

First, In ascertaining the supposed remains of an oracular temple, vestiges of the *adytum*, would be an object of particular research: and perhaps such may be discovered in that part of Mr. Horneman's description, where he mentions *the different levels of the basement or floor of the ancient edifice at Siwah.*

Hen. Steph. in Thesaur. art. " *Adytum*," ἄδυ]ον, locus secretior templi, ad quem non nisi sacerdotibus dabatur accessus, nam ex eo oracula reddebantur.

The *adytum*, was not only a recess, rendered secret by the reve-
rential awe which forbad approach of the vulgar; but was actually
a kind of *crypt*, or place of concealment : among the prodigies fore-
running the victories of Cæsar in Asia, " Pergami in *occultis* ac
remotis templi, quæ Græci ἄδυῖα appellant, tympana sonuêre. Bell.
Civil. lib. iii. cap. 105.

In the itinerary of Pausanias, the ἄδυῖα of the oracular temples
appear to have been sunk beneath, and under the basement or floor
of the building. This was so generally the case, that in *Bœoticis*, the
word *adytum* is used as synonymous for the *cave* of Trophonius. *In
Corinthracis, cap.* i. the entrance and passage to the adytum of
Palæmon at Chronium, is represented as subterraneous ; ἔςι δὲ καὶ
ἄλλο ἄδυῖον καλέμενον, κάθοδος δὲ ἐς αὐῖὸ ὑπὸ γεως. edit. Kuhn. p. 113, and
in the *Achaicis*, the entrance of the adytum of the temple of Minerva,
at Pellené, is from under the base of the statue of the goddess,
and the recess is hyperbolically represented, as penetrating to the
very centre of the earth.

The purposes of these crypts, or concealed recesses in the oracular temples, may readily be surmised : and to conduct their oracle
with proper mystery and imposition of respect, is was a necessary
policy in the priesthood, to prevent any visit or examination of these
hallowed places : the hand of the deity was denounced as punishing
the trespasser with instant death. Of the many examples that offer,
we will take one from *Egypt :* Pausanias in *Phocicis*, mentions,
"That a Roman Prefect having from impious curiosity, sent a
person to inspect the *adytum* of Isis at Coptos, the unhallowed
intruder was struck dead on the spot.

The oracle was given *ex adyto.*

—— isque adytis hæc tristia dicta reportat.        Virg. Æn. l. ii. v. 115.

It was given too *imo adyto,* or as others express it, from the *depth* of the adytum.

Nec dum etiam responsa Deûm monitusque vetusti
Exciderant, voxque ex adytis accepta *profundis*
Prima,——" Lycurge dabis Dircæo funera bello."
                                              Stat. Theb. l. v. 645.

Diod. Sic. lib. xvii. says, that when Alexander required an oracle from Ammon, the chief priest retired back to the sanctuary or holy place, and gave the answer, *ex adyto;* so the Latin version of Wesselingius expresses it: in truth, there is no Greek word in the original, immediately corresponding with *ex adyto;* yet the priest retiring εις σήκον, *i. e.* to the fane or secret recess of the temple; his giving the oracle from such secret recess may be implied.

Applying the accounts of the *adytum* to the building under consideration, it may be observed, that to form such recess, the rock rising in the centre of the enclosure described at Siwah, offered a peculiar accommodation to the architect. The soil around is represented as wet and marshy, and not therefore suited to excavation. The erecting the Προναὸς, or forepart of the temple, on the elevation of the rock, admitted of the interior end or *penetrale* being built over a crypt, or artificial cave of eight feet deep, suitable to the purpose and mysteries of an oracular temple.

The entrance to the ancient edifice described by Mr. Horneman was to the north; and from the northern end or division of the building there was a descent of eight feet, in coming to the southern or interior extremity.

Whether anciently the pavement was level and continued, "covering *the adytum* as a cave;" or whether it was an open vault or recess, from which the priest (as mentioned by Diodorus) might utter the predictions of the oracle unseen by the vulgar; in either case the construction may agree with the ideas to be derived from ancient authority, of the oracular Fane of Ammon ; and more strongly warrant a conjecture, that the ruins described by Horneman, may be those of that renowned temple.

Secondly, Mr. Horneman, observing on the rude and stupendous architecture of the building at Siwah, says, " *that he could in no part discover any mark or trace on the walls, of their having been incrusted or lined with marbles, or of any ornament having been once affixed.*" Indeed the building appears not to have been large, and could little admit of such.

Niches, or pedestals were not required; the most ancient Egyptian temples had no statues: Lucian says,—τὸ δὲ παλαιὸν καὶ παρὰ Αἰγυπ]ίοισι αξόανοι νηοὶ ἔσαν· edit. Bourdelot. p. 1057. The sole interior decoration of the ancient Egyptian temple at Heliopolis, described by Strabo, was a rude sculpture on the walls in the *old Tuscan* taste, apparently similar to that observed by Mr. Horneman on the walls at Siwah. Strabo's words are,—ἀναγλυφὰς δ' ἔχυσιν οἱ τοῖχοι οὗ]οι μεγάλων εἰδώλων ὁμοίων ]οῖς Τυρρενικοῖς, καὶ ]οῖς ἀρχαίοις σφόδρα των παρὰ ]οῖς Ελλησὶ δημιεργηνμά]ων· edit. Casaub. p. 806. This, and the indications of rude simplicity observable in the remains of the ancient building at Siwah, may thus strengthen the conjecture that it was the one sacred to Ammon. Diodorus, Arrian, and Curtius, all indeed talk of gold and ornaments, and even of a statue in procession, displayed on the visit of Alexander: but Strabo directly taxes Callisthenes (and therewith those writers who followed him) with

exaggerations and additions, introduced to do honour to their hero.
Edit. Casaub. p. 813.

The poet Lucan, in his description of the Temple (and its being
a *fiction* will be taken *in aid of the argument*), states the people of
Lybia to be " *beati*," i. e. *rich*; and he had all the gold of Africa before him, if the general account and actual knowledge of this temple
at the time he wrote, could have bore him out in a luxuriant description of its splendour and magnificence. From this he appears to
have abstained, in deference to fact and to what was generally
known, of the *rudeness and simplicity* of this holy place. His being
a poet thus strengthens his authority, whilst he *foregoes the splendour
of description specially suited to his genius*; and gives up matter too
of fine poetical contrast, with the simple and pure morals and religion of his Cato. He had no other inducement but truth when he
says,

> " Non illic Libycæ posuerunt ditia gentes
> Templa, nec Eöis splendent donaria gemmis
> Quamvis Æthiopum populis Arabumque *Beatis*
> Gentibus, atque Indis, unus sit Jupiter Ammon :
> *Pauper adhuc deus est ;* nullis violata per ævum
> Divitiis delubra tenens, morumque priorum
> Numen Romano templum defendit ab auro."
>
> Lucan, lib. ix.

The Temple of Ammon further may be presumed, to have been
of small dimension. When Alexander alone enters the building, it
is mentioned by his historians, that such exclusive permission was a
mark of high respect; but Strabo further informs us, that all who
attended on Alexander, " *heard* the Oracle *from without:*" ἔξωθεν ʼε
ʼῆς θεμεςείας ΑΚΡΟΑΣΑΣΘΑΙ ϖάνʼας πλὴν Ἀλεξάνδρ૪, Τ૪ʼον δ᾽ ἔνδοθεν
ἐῖναι. edit. Casaub. p. 814. The Oracle given from the extreme
recess of the interior, (to which the priest retired for the purpose,

as before cited from Diodorus), could be heard and distinguished from without, only under supposition, that the entrance was at no great distance from the adytum, and the temple, of course, not large.

Thirdly, It is exclusively stated by Mr. Horneman, that *the building at Siwah is situated in the centre of an inclosure, surrounded at some distance by ancient foundations of a strong and massive wall.* Not to lengthen this note by unnecessary citations, it may be sufficient to refer generally to the Itinerary of Pausanias, wherein scarcely a temple is mentioned throughout Greece, without noticing, at the same time its inclosure and circumvallation: and even the sacred grove, distinctively from the temple, was often surrounded by a wall, as was that of Venus *in Eliacis,* cap. xxv.

These walls may be considered, in one respect, as marking the boundary of the holy ground; but further, they were built with a view to protecting not only the sanctity, but the wealth too of the temple.

The statues were often of gold and ivory; and the offerings of golden shields and goblets, and other votive presents, given by those who consulted the oracles, formed a treasure considerable in proportion to the character and renown of the sacred place. Cicero, in his accusation of Verres, notices that the treasures of a state were often deposited too in sanctuaries, not only as protected by the abhorrence of sacrilege, but by the strength of the place: thus the general subsidies collected by the Athenians, at the close of the Persian wars, were kept in the Parthenon; and the wealth pillaged from the temple at Phocis, by Philomelus, and which occasioned the holy war, was immense. On these accounts the greater temples were often placed in actual fortresses. The Temple of Minerva at Syracuse, was in the Ortygia; the Parthenon of Athens, in the Acropolis; the Roman Temple of Jupiter, in the Capitol; and the Editor, when in Sicily, remarked the circumvallations inclosing the temples at Selinunté, and the almost impregnable situations of those at Agrigentum and Segesté.

The foundations of ancient circumvallation at Siwah may thus be considered, in some degree, as indications of the origin and purpose of the building within the inclosure.

The Ammonian temple was certainly surrounded by a strong wall; " triplici muro circumdatum," as Diodorus, lib. xvii. and Q. Curtius, lib. iv. cap. 7, both inform us. Curtius uses the word *munitio*, and the 'Aκρόπολις, *or arx* of Diodorus, answers in description to the mount of Siwah itself; and the temple of Ammon being represented as being erected within the third or more distant inclosure of wall, its distance from the citadel may well correspond *with that* of the ruins in question, from the town of Siwah.

Horneman further informs us, that the ancient building which he describes, stood in the *centre* of the area, and partly on a rock; and at the same time observes, that the ground generally throughout the area was broken and dug up in search of treasure; from which may be inferred that formerly there were *other buildings* within the inclosure. On this head it is almost unnecessary to cite ancient authorities; it will appear from a view of the well known ruins in Greece, Sicily, and the Magna Græcia, &c. that the ancients often availed themselves of one and the same circumvallation, and erected different temples within the general inclosure; so, in the Achaicis of Pausanias, cap. cxx. the temples of Minerva and of Diana Laphia are within the same boundary of wall, without enumerating the many other instances in that curious journal; or to the three temples actually remaining at Pæstum, &c. within the inclosure of one and the same wall. In reference to the subject more immediately under consideration, the *Ammonian temples.of Juno and Mercury* were in high repute with the Greeks, as mentioned in the Eliacis, p. 416, edit. Kuhn: and these temples were probably within the same inclosure as that of Ammon. The temple of Ammon being the principal, might be supposed to be erected in the *centre* and *on the rock*, which strong foundation may have in part yet preserved it, whilst the foundations of the others more easily dug and broken up, have brought those edifices low to the ground; and hence the very materials (as we are told) have been carried away, and no vestiges remain but of the area of the earth having been disturbed and heaped, as the work of search, dilapidation, and pillage was carried on.

Fourthly, Mr. Horneman was shewn, at the distance of half a mile from the ruins, " *a spring of fresh water, which takes its rise in a grove of date trees, and in a most romantic and beautiful situation.*"

This description precisely answers to that of the *Fountain of the Sun*, mentioned by ancient writers : and the distance from the chief temple too, seems to agree. " Haud procul arce *extrinsecùs* alterum Hammonis fanum jacet, quod multæ arbores proceræ inumbrant, et *fons proximus est,* ὀνομαζομένη Ἡλίε κρήνη." Diod. Sic. Tom. II. p. 199. So too Curtius, " Est etiam aliud Hammonis nemus; in medio habet fontem; *Aquam Solis* vocant." Lib. iv. cap. 7.

Thus far the merely descriptive accounts agree. If a further point can be ascertained, it will be conclusive, and the beautiful spot visited by our traveller, be identified as that of the Fountain of the Sun, situated *extrinsecùs,* or without the inclosure, in which stood the principal temple of Ammon.

The water of the Fountain of the Sun was, at different periods of each twenty-four hours, successively *hot* and *cold:* " Aquam enim habet, cum horis diei miris subinde vicibus re variantem. Nam sub lucis ortum tepidam emittit. Die hinc progrediente pro horarum suc- cedentium ratione, frigescit. Sub æstum vero meridianum frigedo ejus summa est. Quæ rursùs parili modo remittit usque ad vesperam. Tunc appetente nocte rursùs incalescit, ad mediam usque noctem, ubi exæstuat. Exinde calor sensìm deficit: donec unà cum exortâ luce pristinam teporis vicem recuperârit." Diod. Sic. Tom. II. edit. Wesseling, p. 199.

Mr. Horneman appears to have made no inquiries on this curious subject; but tells us, that having asked, " if there was any spring of fresh water near ?" he was shewn to the one he describes, un- doubtedly the *nearest,* and probably the same as seen by Mr. Brown, who says, ( p. 24 of his Volume of Travels), " that one of the springs which rise near the ruins described, is observed by the natives, to be *sometimes cold and sometimes warm."* Mr. Brown does not appear to have considered the Oasis of Siwah as that of Ammon. He had no favourite discovery to set forth and confirm by parti- cular remarks and circumstances: he had not an interest in his account of the changeable temperature of this spring, but that of truth. The periodical variation from hot to cold, and from cold to heat, may rather, therefore on his relation, be assumed as fact; and be taken as a matter of proof concurrent with the grove, the spring itself, the distance from the ruins, and the beauty of the situation, *all* answering to the descriptions of the *Fountain of the Sun,* given by ancient writers, and, in reference to the ruins, rendering the conjecture more probable, that they are those of the Temple of Ammon.

Fifthly, Mr. Horneman says, " that the material of which the building is constructed, is a limestone, containing *petrifactions of shells and small marine animals ;* and that such stone is *to be found and dug up in the neighbourhood :"* so too Strabo tells us, p. 49, that sea fossils and shells were spread on the Oasis of Ammon ; κα]α]ὴν μεσόγαιαν ὁρᾶ]αι ϖολλαχϗ κόχλων καὶ ὀςρέων καὶ χηραμίδων πλῆϑος, καὶ λιμνοθάλα]τοι καθάπερ φησὶ περὶ ]ὸ ἱερον ]ϗ Ἄμμωνος. Strabo, p. 50, further noticing the marine substances scattered on the Oasis of Ammon, cites Eratosthenes, supposing that the sea once reached to that interior spot of Africa, and supporting his conjecture by observing, that the oracle could not anciently, and in the first instance, have been so renowned and visited, if difficult of access, by being far *inland.* Casaubon's version expresses it, " fortassis etiam Ammonis templum, aliquando in mari jacuisse, quod nunc maris effluxu sit in mediâ terrâ ; ac conjicere se, oraculum illud optimâ ratione tam illustre ac celebre factum, esse quòd in mari esset situm, neque ejus gloriam probabile esse tantam potuisse existere, quanta nunc est, si tam longè fuisset a mari dissitum." P. 50. The poet follows the geographer's idea, and derives a fine sentiment for the mouth of Cato.

Numen ————————————————————
——————————— steriles nec legit arenas,
Ut caneret paucis, mersitque hoc pulvere verum.
Pharsal. lib. ix. v. 576.

Now, taking the simple fact, the stones with which the Temple of Ammon was built, might be supposed to contain *fragments of marine animals and shells,* such as those mentioned by Horneman. For the rest, Strabo's (or rather Eratosthene's) conjecture is scarcely admissible.

The Libyan Ammon had long been venerated in Greece, and throughout the then civilized world. A subordinate temple was consecrated to Ammon in Laconia, and the god was yet more anciently worshipped by the Aphytæi. Paus. Kuhn, p. 293. Another temple was raised to Ammon in Bœotia, and in which Pindar dedicated a statue of the god ; and the same great poet wrote a hymn to the Lybian deity, and sent the copy to its priesthood in Africa. Bœotica, p. 741. So anciently and so highly as the oracle of Ammon was revered, and so much as it was resorted to by the most enlightened nations of Greece, Asia, and Egypt, the circumstance of its once having been situated on the coasts of the sea, could not have escaped tradition or direct historical account, if such had ever been the fact.

The above remarks are with deference submitted to the reader, as adding probability to the conjecture, that the ruins seen by Mr. Horneman, in the vicinity of Siwah, may be the actual remains of the *ancient oracular temple of Ammon.*

Having in the above comment cited a passage from the *Pharsalia,* not as authority, but for purpose of inference ; and having further adverted to a sentiment attributed to the philosophic hero of the poem, in reference to the inland and sequestered situation of the temple of Ammon ; the annotator is induced to close this essay with a version of the admirable speech of Cato at length, as deriving a peculiar interest from connection with the subject under discussion, appearing to terminate, (and leave as it were, in ruins,) the superstitions of the oracle, with the fabric of its temple.

Lucan tells us, that Cato approaching the Fane of Jupiter Ammon in Lybia, was requested by Labienus to demand of the oracle,—" What was to be the fate of Cæsar ?—whether Rome was to be enslaved or free ?—and in what consisted virtue, &c. &c."

Cato, (his spirit flaming high, as e'er·
From Ammon's fane burst forth in prophecy)—
Spoke from his heart,—the sacred shrine of truth !—
" What would thou, Labienus ?—should I ask,
If being free, that freedom I'd resign ?
If I would die,—before I'd be a slave ?
If life is nought,—when measur'd but by years ?
If evil can affect the good ;—or whether
The threat of Fortune's lost upon the brave ?
If to deserve well is enough ?—or if,
Desert is yet dependant on success ?
All this I know :—Ammon can't tell ME more !
We all depend on God :—(his priest and oracle
Silent) His will is known, nor does he need
A voice, but that within the breast of man :
Our duties are implanted on our births !
The God of Nature ne'er confin'd his lessons
Here, to the few ;—or buried his great truths
In Afric's sands.——Is not HIS HOLY PLACE,—
At once all earth, sea, air, and heav'n, and virtue ?—
God is, whate'er we see,—where'er we move !
Let those who doubt, go ask at yonder fane
Their lot ?—not knowing how they'd act, or feel.
No oracle confirms, or moves, *my* thoughts ;
—Makes nought more rare :—I know I am to die,
And this doth make me sure,—of how to live !
The coward and the brave, the bad and good
Alike must die !—and God declaring this,
Made known to man, all man requires to know !"
    Thus Cato spoke,—turn'd from the hallow'd fane
In faith and virtue satisfied ; and left
Ammon, to Ammon's votaries,——the people.

W. Y.

*Ille Deo plenus, tacitâ quem mente gerebat,*
*Effudit dignas adytis è pectore voces :*
*" Quid quæri, Labiene, jubes ?—an liber in armis*
*Occubuisse velim potiùs, quàm regna videre ?*
*An sit vita nihil, sed longam differat ætas ?*
*An noceat vis ulla bono ?—Fortunaque perdat*
*Oppositâ virtute minas,—laudandaque velle*
*Sit satis, et nunquam successu crescat honestum ?*
*Scimus ; et hoc nobis non altiùs inseret Ammon.*
*Hæremus cuncti Superis, temploque tacente,*
*Nil facimus non sponte Dei : nec vocibus ullis*
*Numen egit : dixitque semel nascentibus auctor*
*Quicquid scire licet ; steriles nec legit arenas*
*Ut caneret paucis, mersitque hoc pulvere verum.*
*Estne Dei sedes, nisi terra, et pontus, et aër,*
*Et cælum, et virtus ? Superos quid quærimus ultrà ?*
*Juppiter est quodcunque vides, quocumque moveris !*
*Sortilegis egeant dubii, semperque futuris*
*Casibus ancipites : me non oracula certum,*
*Sed mors certa facit : pavido, fortique cadendum est.*
*Hoc satis est dixisse Jovem." Sic ille profatur*
*Servatâque fide, templi discedit ab aris,*
*Non exploratum populis Ammona relinquens.*

Lucan. lib. ix. v. 564.

# POSTSCRIPT.

# POSTSCRIPT.

It may be satisfactory to his Employers and to the Public, to receive some further account of Mr. Horneman, on termination of the travels more immediately the subject of his Journal.

By a letter from Mr. Horneman, dated at Tripoly, August 19, 1799, it appears, that on coming to Mourzouk, the end of October, 1798, he was informed that a caravan was preparing to set out for Soudan in three divisions, of which the first was to depart in three days after his arrival. The period fixed for departure of the last division, allowed time for the necessary preparations, and Mr. Horneman had intended to proceed with it on a journey to the Agades and Cashna; but informations he afterwards received induced him to alter his purpose. He was told that the caravan was likely to meet with obstruction or attack in passing through a country of the Tauricks, then at war with Fezzan; and he observed that the caravan consisted wholly of black traders, from whose intercourse or connection he was not likely to derive either useful consequence or patronage, which might facilitate his friendly reception with the Moors of interior Africa. These and other circumstances induced him to forego the present opportunity, and with the less regret, as, at no distant period, a great caravan was expected from Bornou, with which, on its return, he might travel to the greatest advantage. Whilst remaining at Mourzouk, himself and his servant Frendenburgh were seized with the country fevers: Horneman recovered, but his servant died.

On the re-establisment of his health, Horneman found that some months yet must elapse before the caravan could be expected from Bornou : and in the interval of public resort from the arrival or passage of the caravans, Mourzouk affording no further objects of curiosity or interest, he determined to proceed to Tripoly, for the purpose of transmitting to the Committee of the African Association, such intelligence as he had hitherto collected in their service. He arrived at Tripoly, after a journey of two months, about the middle of August; transacted the business he had in view, and on the 1st of December, 1799, set out on his return to Mourzouk, where he arrived January 20th, 1800.

Two letters from Mourzouk have been since received, and at date of writing the last, Mr. Horneman was on *the eve of setting out with the caravan for Bornou;* and with intention from that remote kingdom to prosecute further discoveries to the westward, and in the heart of Africa.

The letters from Mourzouk are as follow :

" SIR,                                  " *Mourzouk, February* 20, 1800.

" I left Tripoly the 1st of December, 1799, and arrived here (the capital of Fezzan) January 20th, 1800, after a safe and good journey, though protracted and slow. I am in the best health, and with fair probability of its continuance.

" The route from hence to Soudan, is not yet secure enough for me to undertake proceeding by way of the Agades.

" There is now at this place, a Shereef of Bornou, a man of sense, and very much considered by the Sultan of that country. I have made him my friend, and it is in his company I shall depart from this place about the 15th of March for Bornou, whence in the months of August or September, I think to reach Cashna, distant from Bornou about fifteen days journey.

" I shall write as often as opportunity offers, that at least some letters may arrive for your information, and the tranquillity of my family.

" I remain, with great esteem,

" SIR,

" Your most obedient,

" FREDERICK HORNEMAN."

*Right Hon. Sir Joseph Banks, K. B.*
*President of the Royal Society, &c.*

" SIR,                                     " *Mourzouk, April 6, 1800.*

" Our caravan is on the point of setting off for Bornou, myself shall join it in the evening.

" Being in an excellent state of health, perfectly inured to the climate, sufficiently acquainted with the manners of my fellow-travellers, speaking the Arabic language, and somewhat of the Bornou tongue, and being well armed and not without courage, and under protection of two great Shereefs, I have the best hopes of success in my undertaking.

" The Soudan caravan left this place about a month ago; I did well not to join it, as some time past a number of Tibbo were seen hovering, with an intention of attacking that caravan.

" Being the first European traveller undertaking so long a journey
in this part of the world, *I will not put my discoveries to the hazard,
by exposing myself to the casualties of long and unnecessary residence
and delays in any one place,* and propose staying no longer at Bornou
than till the month of September, when I shall proceed to Cashna
with the great caravan, which always about that time of the year
sets out from Bornou for Soudan.

" I cannot yet decide on my further procedure on leaving Soudan,
or Cashna, but you may depend on my best intentions and wishes
to give full satisfaction to the Society.

" Consider this letter as the last for this year, or perhaps as the
last before my arrival at some port on the coast of Africa.   March
the 24th I sent a long letter from Tripoly, and being by a good
opportunity, have no doubt of its arriving safe.*

" In addition to what I stated in my letter of the 24th of March,
I have to observe, that in the small-pox, the application used here to
preserve the eyes of children, consists of what they term *samsuc,*
(tamarinds,) and *zurenbula zigollan,* (onions,) and this with good
effect, as I am told.

" I have more particularly made inquiry respecting venereal disorders, and can confirm what I before wrote, that salts and colo-
quintida, (in Arabic *handal)* are specific remedies for that disease
in this country, and used in the manner I described.

" From every information I can collect, the natives of Fezzan are
not susceptible of venereal infection more than once in their lives.
It is singular, that notwithstanding there is a great difference as to

* It never came to hand.

the nature of this disease, between poxes brought here by the caravan from Soudan, and by those from Tripoly and Cairo, yet never (or at least very seldom,) can a man get these two sorts one after the other in the course of his life.

" Some days past I spoke to a man who had seen Mr. Brown in Darfoor; he gave me some information respecting the countries he travelled through, and told me, that the communication of the Niger with the Nile was not to be doubted, but that this communication before the rainy season was very little in those parts ; the Niger being at the dry period reposing, or *non fluens.*

" Not long ago, the same custom was observed at Bornou as in ancient times at Cairo, ' a girl very richly dressed, was thrown into the river Niger.'

" Comparing my enquiries as to Soudan, and its communication with the western and south-western coasts of Africa, it must lay generally by the way of Nyffé and Jerba, and be twelve times greater than that between Fezzan and Soudan.

" I recommend myself to your remembrance, and assuring you of my great esteem, am

" Sir,

" Your most obedient,

" FREDERICK HORNEMAN."

*Right Hon. Sir Joseph Banks, K. B.*
*President of the Royal Society, &c.*

Mr. Horneman, previous to setting out for Bornou, had availed himself of the intimacies he had formed with intelligent pilgrims and merchants of the Egyptian caravan, and with others at Mourzouk, who were natives of, or had traded to, different regions of Africa, to collect every possible information respecting the countries he was about to visit; and, together with his Journal, transmitted the following result of his enquiries.

# INTELLIGENCE

## CONCERNING THE

## INTERIOR PART OF NORTH AFRICA.

---

## SECTION I.

WESTWARD from Fezzan, and to the south and south-west, the country is inhabited by the Tibbo, who command also the country from Fezzan towards Egypt, from which it is said to be separated by a large desert. The nearest inhabited places north of Tibbo are Ungila and Supah. On the south they are bounded by wandering Arabs ; and on the west beyond Fezzan, by the dominions of the Tuaricks.

The Tibbo are not quite black ; their growth is slender ; their limbs are well turned ; their walk is light and swift ; their eyes are quick, their lips thick, their nose is not turned up, and not large ; their hair is very long, but less curled than that of the Negroes. They appear to have much natural capacity, but they have too few opportunities of improving it, being surrounded by barbarous nations, or Mahometans. Their intercourse with the Arabs, to whom they convey slaves, has probably corrupted them ; they are accused of being mistrustful, treacherous, and deceitful. The Fezzanians do not travel singly with them, for they are afraid of being surprised and murdered at the instigation of the company with whom they travel. The language of the Tibbo is spoken with extraordinary rapidity, and has many consonants, particularly the L and S. They number thus :

| One, | *Trono.* |
|------|----------|
| Two, | ———. |
| Three, | *Agesso.* |
| Four, | *Fusso.* |
| Five, | *Fo.* |
| Ten, | *Markum.* |

Their cloathing consists of sheep-skins, which they dress with or without the wool; the former for winter, the latter for summer; but the inhabitants of the principal places, or others, when they go to Fezzan, clothe themselves like the Burmuans, in large blue shirts; their head is wrapt in a dark blue cloth in such a manner, that their eyes only are seen. Their weapons are a lance about six feet long, and a knife from fifteen to twenty inches long, which they carry on their left arm, the sheath being fastened to a ring of leather about three inches wide, which they bear on their wrist.

The Tibbo are divided into several tribes, the principal of which are, the Tibbo of Bilma, whose chief resides at Dyrke, about one day's journey from Bilma. This tribe is a good deal mixed, having established itself forcibly among the Negroes who lived in that district: to this day, the inhabitants of Bilma are mostly Negroes; in Dyrke, on the contrary, they are Tibbo. This tribe carries on a commerce between Fezzan and Burnu, and apparently with great safety to themselves; for they travel in small companies of six or eight men; but on account of their bad character, the slaves of either sex, from Burnu, who have been freed, do not return with them, as the poor people are afraid of being plundered and sold again, or murdered by them.

The religion of the Tibbo of Bilma, is the Mahometan ; but it is said they hold it very cheap.

The tribe of the Tibbo Rschade, or the Rock Tibbo, is so called from their houses being built under rocks, and they frequently live even in caves, before which they build huts of rushes in a very coarse manner, for their summer residence. The chief of this tribe lives in Abo ; next to which Tibesty is the largest place. The Tibbo Rschade go in multitudes to Fezzan, at which time they clothe themselves like the Tuarick ; however, I have seen several wearing their sheep-skins. This tribe is reported to be good Mahometans.

The Tibbo Burgu are said to be still Pagans : the district which they inhabit, abounds in dates, corn, and grass.

A company of Fezzanians having this year been plundered by some of the people of Burnu, as they were travelling from Bergami to Mourzouk, the sultan of Fezzan sent a small army into their country : it consisted of thirty-two men on horseback, seventy Arabs on foot, and about two hundred Tibbos of the Rschade tribe. The Arabs went from Mourzouk into Gatron, fifty-four miles south of that place ; to Fegherie thirty-three miles south-south-west of Gatron ; then to Abo seven days, and Tibesty three days, in an easterly direction ; then to Burgu eighteen days, (reckoning a day's journey eighteen miles.) They stole about two hundred people, the greatest part of whom were sold in a treacherous manner.

The women of the Burgu tribe, wear their hair in plaits, which hang down from their heads, but the hair on the fore-part of their heads is cut off. The girls are accused of becoming pregnant by their brothers. The slave of one of my friends, who spoke the Tibbo language, assured me, that he had questioned a young woman who was with child, and that she did not deny it.

Farther towards the east lies Arna, the principal place of another Tibbo tribe, at the distance of five or six days.

South-south-west of Augila dwell the Febabo, who are exposed to the yearly depredations of the Arabs of Bengasi, who go out with the Arabs of Augila, to steal men and dates ; and for that purpose, they convey with them several hundred camels.

The distance to Febabo was stated to me by the Augilarians to be ten days journey, (twenty-one miles per day,) and that during the first six days no water is to be found. The most southerly of the Tibbo tribes are the Nomadic Tibbo, who live in the *Bahr-el-Gasel*, which is said to be a long and fruitful valley, seven days journey from Bergami northward.

## SECTION II.

THE west and south of Fezzan is inhabited by the Tuarick, a mighty people, who border south-west on Burnu; south on Burnu, Soudan, and Tombuctoo; eastward on the country of the Tibbo and Fezzan; northward on part of Fezzan, and the Arabs who live behind the regions of Tripoly, Tunis, and Algiers ; and westward on the great empire of Fez and Morocco, of whom a few colonies

are found in Sockna, (in the dominion of Fezzan), Augila, and
Siwah; in which places the language of the Tuarick is the only
one spoken by the inhabitants.*

The Tuarick are divided into many nations and tribes, who all
speak the same language; but, by their colour and manner of living,
it is probable that they differ widely in their origin.  As I will give
only certain informations, on this account I confine myself, in the
following relation, to the Tuarick of the nation of Kolluvi and the
tribe of Hagara.  These are thin in growth, rather tall than short;
their walk is swift but firm; their look is stern, and their whole
demeanour is warlike.  Cultivated and enlightened, their natural
abilities would render them, perhaps, one of the greatest nations
upon earth.  Their character (particularly that of Kolluvi,) is much
esteemed.  The western tribes of this nation are white, as much as
the climate and manner of living will admit.  The Kolluvians who
reached the region of Asben and conquered Agades, and mixed with
the nations, are of different colours; many of them are black; but
their features are not like those of Negroes.  The Hagara and
Matkara are yellowish, like the Arabs; near Soudan there are tribes
entirely black.  The clothing of this nation consists of wide dark-
blue breeches, a short narrow shirt of the same colour, with wide
sleeves, which they bring together and tie on the back of their
neck, so that their arms are at liberty.  They wind a black cloth
round their head in such a manner that at a distance it appears
like a helmet, for their eyes only are seen.  Being Mahometans,
they cut off their hair, but leave some on the top of the head,
round which those who wear no cap, contrive to fold their black
cloth, so that it appears like a tuft on their helmet.  Round their

* I have given further particulars on this subject in the account of my journey
from Cairo to Fezzan.

waist they wear a girdle of a dark colour; from several cords which fall from their shoulders, hangs a koran in a leather pouch, and a row of small leather bags containing amulets. They always carry in their hands a small lance, neatly worked, about five feet long. Above the left elbow, on the upper part of the arm, they wear their national badge, a thick, black or dark-coloured ring, of horn or stone.

Their upper dress is a Soudanian shirt, over which a long sword hangs from the shoulder. The travelling merchants of this nation carry fire-arms; the others use only the sword, the lance, and the knife, which they carry on their left arm, like the Tibbo, but the handle is finely worked; for they have the art of giving to copper as bright a colour as the English artists, and this art they keep very secret.

They carry on a commerce between Soudan, Fezzan, and Gadames. Their caravans give life to Mourzouk, which, without them, is a desert; for they, like the Soudanians, love company, song and music.

The Tuarick are not all Mahometans. In the neighbourhood of Soudan and Tombuctoo live the Tagama, who are white, and of the Pagan religion. This must have occasioned the report, to which my attention has been called, by several learned men, that there are white Christians in the neighbourhood of Tombuctoo. I am convinced that the fable arises solely from the expression *Nazary* (i. e. Christians), which the Arabs and Mahometans use in general for unbelievers.

The greatest part of the eastern Tuarick lead a wandering life.

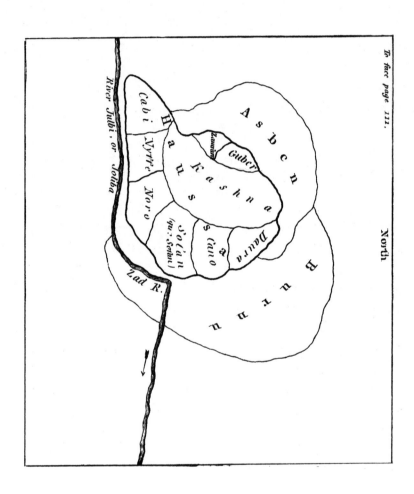

North

River Julbi, or Joliba

Cabi

Nyffe

Noro

Zad R.

Haussa

Zamiara

Guber

Kashna

Daura

S'o'da'n
(qu.: Sudan)

Cano

Asben

Burnu

A place, for instance, under the government of Hagara consists of about twenty-five or thirty stone houses only; but at the time of their markets (which are said to be very considerable), many hundred men assemble there with their leathern tents.

## SECTION III.

BEHIND these countries lies Tombuctoo, of which I shall say nothing, as I could not get any well-founded and certain accounts, for there is little intercouse between this region and Fezzan; however, it certainly is the most remarkable and principal town in the interior of Africa.

Eastward from Tombuctoo lies Soudan, Haussa, or Asna; the first is the Arabic, the second is the name used in the country, and the last is the Burnuan name. Of these three names I choose the second, as being the most proper, and understood by the Arabs below Soudan, and all the land southward from Ghaden. The Burnuan name means properly only Kano and Kashna, and the country lying eastward from that region Asna, but incorrectly spoken, it comprehends also Tombuctoo.

As to what the inhabitants themselves call Haussa, I had, as I think, very certain information. One of them, a Marabut, gave me a drawing of the situation of the different regions bordering on each other, which I here give as I received it. (See the Sketch opposite.)

The land within the strong line is Haussa; my black friend had added Asben.

These regions are governed by Sultans, of whom those of Kashna and Kano are the most powerful; but they all (either by constraint or policy) pay tribute to Burnu, except Cabi or Nyffé, their districts being at too great a distance. Guber pays, moreover, a tribute to Asben. Zamtara is united with Guber; the Sultan of the latter having taken possession of it, killed the Sultan, and sold all the prisoners he could take.

The Haussa are certainly Negroes, but not quite black; they are the most intelligent people in the interior of Africa; they are distinguished from their neighbours by an interesting countenance; their nose is small and not flattened, and their stature is not so disagreeable as that of the Negroes, and they have an extraordinary inclination for pleasure, dancing, and singing. Their character is benevolent and mild. Industry and art, and the cultivation of the natural productions of the land, prevail in their country; and, in this respect, they excel the Fezzanians, who get the greatest part of their clothes and houshold implements from the Soudanians. They can dye in their country any colour but scarlet. The culture of their land is as perfect as that of the Europeans, although the manner of doing it is very troublesome. In short, we have very unjust ideas of this people, not only with respect to their cultivation and natural abilities, but also of their strength and the extent of their possessions, which are by no means so considerable as they have been represented. Their music is imperfect, when compared to the European; but the Haussanian women have skill enough to affect their husbands, thereby even to weeping, and to inflame their courage to the greatest fury against their enemies. The public singers are called Kadanka.

## SECTION IV.

EASTWARD from Haussa are situated the dominions of the Sultan of Burnu (*i. e.* the city). It appears to be much increased since the time of Leo Africanus, as other regions belong to it, which he considered as independent; for example, Wangara, also Edrisi's Cauga, &c. belong to it.

The Sultan of Burnu is reckoned the most powerful in that district; all the neighbouring states pay him tribute. He certainly possesses an extensive tract of land, but he gains more by his authority in the unceasing animosity of his neighbours.

The Burnuans are blacker than the Haussanians, and completely Negroes; they are stronger, and very patient of labour; their constitution is in the greatest degree phlegmatic; they are, altogether, much more rude and uninformed than the Haussanians. Their men are fond of women only of a large size; the Soudanians, on the contrary, prefer those of a slender form.

A paste made of flour and flesh is the only food of the Burnuans; the liquor they drink is an intoxicating kind of beer, which is very nourishing. The best natural production of Burnu is copper, which is said to be found in small native pieces. That which is gold in Tombuctoo and Haussa, is answered by copper in Burnu; the value of all their commodities is fixed by pounds of this metal.

Northward from the principal town of that district lies Kanena, which is inhabited by the nation Kojam, so called from their food, which is cow's milk and beef.

Towards the north-east lies Begarmé, the capital of which is called Mesna. Both these territories are dependants of Burnu. Begarmé is famous for its slave trade, perhaps particularly so, as at that place the greatest number of boys are mutilated.

Southward from Burnu lie Margi and Couga; westward, Ungura, (Wangara); they are under the dominion of governors appointed by the Sultan.

## SECTION V.

Towards east by north lies Lussi; by the natives it is called Fiddri, and by the people who dwell eastward, Cougu. The dominions of the Sultan of Fiddri are situated round a lake which bears the same name. This realm was formerly one of the most powerful, now it is considerably diminished, by the treachery of the Sultans of Begarmé and Wadey. The natives live in small huts, which they prefer to houses; they are said to be in a very low degree of civilization. There is not any salt in their country, but they procure it in the following manner: they burn a great heap of straw of *gassab*, gather the ashes and put them in a basket, pour water on them, and collect it as it runs through; this water they boil until the salt settles.

Towards the south-east of Fiddri lies Metho, a small independent district in a mountainous country. Eastward lies Wadey, which formerly consisted of several small states, but was conquered by the Arabs, who united and made them one realm. The principal language is Arabic; but above ten other languages are spoken in the district. Wandering Arabs occupy the space from Wadey to Begarmé northward.

Eastward from Wadey lies Darfoor; from whence flows a river, the banks of which are very rich in sugar canes: it runs through Wadey, and falls into the lake Fiddri above-mentioned. I had very different accounts of the circumference of this lake, as in the rainy season it swells to double the extent, which, ordinarily, is from four to eight days journey.

## SECTION VI.

THE river that was seen by Mr. Park on his journey to Tombuctoo, flows southward from Haussa. It waters Nyffé and Cabi, where it is called Julbi; and runs eastward into the district of Burnu, where it takes the name of Zad, which means the great water; in some parts of Haussa, it is called Gaora, or the great water.

All the Burnuans and Haussans whom I questioned about the distant regions of this river, agreed in telling me, " that it ran through the land of Majies, (*i. e.* Heathens;) by Sennaar: others affirmed that it passes Darfoor, in its course eastward, and flows to Cairo, being one stream with the Egyptian Nile."

A native of Egypt from Osuit, who had travelled several times to Darfoor, and southward from that place to collect slaves, and lately returned through Wadey, Fiddri, and Begarmé, to Fezzan, informed me, that the river called *Bab-el-Abiad*, is this river. I could get no intelligence about a great inland lake, although I made every possible inquiry.

Besides these two great rivers here described, there are seven small streams in Haussa, which fall into the Julbi near Berva. Northward from Burnu, there is a river which disappears among the mountains, and is said to rush into the earth. All these rivers are very low in the dry season, and swell amazingly during the rainy season. The breadth of the Zad was given me for one mile, (others said two); but in the rainy season, the breadth is said to be a day's journey, (*i. e.* eight hours). The Budumas always keep themselves in the middle of this stream; they are a very savage, heathenish nation.

These few informations are the best that I have been able to collect, on the interior of Africa. In this relation, I pass over men with tails, without necks, and without hair, without land, and living only on the great sea. It would be an easy matter for me to write you many letters on the interior state of Africa; but I might thereby convey information inaccurate or untrue. Besides, am I not returning to England? and if I do return, should I not reserve something new and interesting to plead my excuse for returning?

If I do not perish in my undertaking, I hope in five years, I shall be able to make the Society better acquainted with the people, of whom I have given this short description.

(Signed)        FREDERICK HORNEMAN.

1798

*Extracts from a Letter accompanying the above Informations, dated Tripoly, 19th of August, 1799.*

" AFTER a journey of eleven days from Siwah, four of which we travelled eighteen hours each day, through a desert, we arrived at Augila, a small miserable town belonging to Tripoly; and after a journey of sixteen days more, we reached Temissa, the first village of Fezzan. Seven of these sixteen days, I was passing a black rocky desert, certainly the worst of all routes in the world; and which has doubtless been formed by some volcanic revolution. It is called Harutsch, and extend very far to the south-west.

" From Temissa, I came by way of Zuila, Tuila, and Tragan, to Mourzouk, (which is also called Fezzan, and by the people of Burnu, *Zela*). Mourzouk is situated in 25° 54' 15" north latitude.

" With regard to the interior of Africa, I have made all the inquiries possible, and will send you the result of them by the first opportunities. Accept for the present the following notices on that subject.

" The river you call Niger—in Soudan, *Gulbi*, or *Gaora*; in Burnu, *Zad*; is a very large river, into which fall more than twelve other rivers. It comes from Tombuctoo, as I am told, runs to the south of Haussa (or Soudan), in the empire of Burnu; here it takes a more southern direction, and falls (at least I could not find a single man who said to the contrary), south of Darfoor into the Nile. There is another river coming from Darfoor, which passes by Wadey and Metho, and terminates in a large lake called *Fiddri,* in a kingdom called by the inhabitants Fiddri; by the people to the east of them, *Cougu;* and by those on the west, *Lussi.* The lake of Fiddri is four days in circumference, but in the time of the rains much more extensive, inundating the surrounding country, which, after the waters are withdrawn, is sown and cultivated.

" Near to *Mesna,* the capital of Bergamé, is another large river; but it is considerable only in the rainy season. Bahr of Gazelles, or *Wad-el-Gazelles,* is not a river, but a long and fertile valley, inhabited by Nomadian Tibbo, whose houses are made of skins.

" *Burnu* is the most powerful kingdom in the interior of Africa. The next to it is the sultan of *Asben,* who resides at Agades. The kings of the countries of which Haussa consists, all pay tribute to Burnu; these are *Kashna, Daura, Keeno, Sofau, Noro, Nyffé, Gaauri, Cabi, Guber,* (Zanfara belongs to Guber.) Kashna pays every year 100 slaves, &c. Some of them pay to Burnu and Asben. The king of Asben with the greatest part of his nation are Tuaricks of the tribe *Kolluvi.* Many of the Tuaricks near to Tombuctoo, are white; and another tribe near to Burnu, are also white, like the Arabs of the northern coast of Africa.

_ " Begarmé pays tribute to Burnu ; *Ungura,* (doubtless *Wangara,* Leo. Afr.) and *Cougu,* are governed by officers of that sultan.

" There is a general opinion of all Burnu and Fezzan people, that Burnu and Fezzan, according to our manner of speaking, lie under the same meridian. Burnu is distant from Kashna 15 days, by travelling very slow 20 fisturnees, or about 330 English miles. Fiddri from Burnu E by N 25 days. The people of Fiddri have no salt in their country, but what they prepare from straw ashes.

" A great part of the people of *Wadey*, together with their king, are Arabs.

" In the direction of south by west from Augila, distant ten days, or about 200 miles, are the *Febabo*, and some days more to the south the *Birgu*, nations of the Tibbo, whose country is very fine and fertile : they are said to be Pagans. It is singular, that the people of Augila, in speaking of these tribes, make much the same comparison which Herodotus (Melpom. c. 183.) does, when speaking of the Ethiopian *Troglodytæ*, hunted by the Garamantes, ' that their language is like the whistling of birds.'

" The most interesting nation of Africa, is the *Tuarick*. (Leo Afr. calls them *Terga*, طرجي.) They are in possession of all the country between Fezzan, Gadames, the empire of Morocco, Tombuctoo, Soudan, Burnu, and the country of the Tibbo. They are divided into several nations, of which the *Kolluvi* in Asben, and the *Hagara* near to Fezzan, are the chief.

" Christians and tailed men, I suppose, never will be found in the interior of Africa. The Mahometans call *Nazari* (which is properly the name for Christians) not the Christians only, but also every other people who are not of their religion. Of tailed men I heard no accounts, except from one person, (but not a *testis fide dignissimus*,) who placed them ten days south of Kano ; he called them *Yem Yem*, and said that they were cannibals. In ten months I shall be near to that direction.

" I shall now, Sir, conclude this letter, which I hope will find you in good health. I am, &c. &c.

" FREDERICK HORNEMAN."

# GEOGRAPHICAL ILLUSTRATIONS

OF

## MR. HORNEMAN'S ROUTE;

AND

## ADDITIONS TO THE GENERAL GEOGRAPHY OF AFRICA.

BY

## MAJOR RENNELL.

# CONSTRUCTION

OF THE

## GEOGRAPHY OF MR. HORNEMAN'S EXPEDITION IN AFRICA.

## CHAPTER I.

In the discussion of the construction of this Geography, I shall confine myself, as much as possible, to general statements; reserving more particular details to a future time, when more materials may arrive: for it is to be observed that although Mr. Horneman has transmitted much valuable matter, yet that it is not altogether of the kind required for the construction of mathematical geography. Fortunately, however, the observations of Mr. Browne and others, enable me to derive more advantage from those of Mr. Horneman, than could have been obtained from them, alone.

The geographical positions of Cairo, Alexandria, and Fezzan, have undergone some small change in the present maps,* in consequence of recent, and it may be supposed, more accurate information. Cairo is placed 2 min. and Alexandria 13, more to the west, in consequence of the French observations: and Mourzouk, the

* The Reader is referred to the Map of Mr. Horneman's Route, page 29, and to the General Map of Africa, opposite Chapter III.

capital of **Fezzan**, 39 G. miles more to the south-east, on a general result of the authorities; amongst which Mr. Horneman's is allowed its due weight. Some other trifling changes have been made, in the positions of Siwah, and of El Bareton, or *Parætonium :* but none of them are more than shades of difference, in respect of the geography at large.

The chief alteration is that of Mourzouk, which, by the former accounts, was said to lie *directly south* from Mesurata: and this alteration is grounded on the line of distance of Mr. Horneman, which does not allow of so great an interval between Egypt and Fezzan, as that position requires, by nearly 25 G. miles; which after all, is no great proportion, in more than 800. It is conceived that Mr. Horneman's *time*, although kept in a coarse way, ought still to be preferred to the mere report of the bearing from Mesurata, on a distance of seventeen or eighteen journies.

I shall begin by tracing in detail the route of Mr. Horneman from Egypt to Fezzan, dividing it into four parts: 1. From Cairo to Siwah: 2. Siwah to Augila: 3. Augila to Fezzan: and 4. Remarks on the position of Mourzouk.

### I. *Cairo to Siwah.*

Mr. Horneman's time may be taken at *about* 123 hours,* which at 2,05 G. miles, the ordinary caravan rate, reduced to direct distance, is equal to 252 G. miles. If taken at $2\frac{1}{2}$ B. miles per hour, which is the ordinary road distance, with an allowance of $\frac{1}{20}$ for inflexions,

* Mr. Horneman had the misfortune to lose his papers at Schiacha, three days beyond Siwah; so that he must have written down the time, previous to that

(the Desert routes are remarkably straight,) we have 255. Now, Mr. Browne's route, along the sea coast from Alexandria, and thence inland from the neighbourhood of *Parætonium,* gives about 259½, or 6½ more than the lowest of these calculations; 4½ more than the highest. Mr. Browne's rout lay first along the coast, 75½ hours; from whence he made a course of about S 19 W (true) 62¼ hours, to Siwah, in the parallel of 29° 12′ by observation. Considering the sinuosities of the coast, which he kept to, almost the whole way, perhaps no more than 144 or 145 G. miles, ought to be allowed in direct distance.

His station on the coast, at about 20 miles east of Parætonium, should be in lat. 31° 7′, according to M. D'Anville; so that the bearing of S 19 W cuts the parallel of Siwah, in longitude 26° 24′: and my former position of it, in the Geography of Herodotus, p. 574, is 26° 21′ 30″. And as Mr. Horneman does not profess to be perfectly accurate in his account of the time, (doubtless because he had lost his papers) I shall adopt the position given by

accident, from recollection only. Between Cairo and Siwah, his time is given, as follows:

| | Hours. |
|---|---|
| Cairo to Wady-el-Latron, or the Natron Valley, *about* – – | 19 |
| To a sand hill, (supposed to be the ridge between the Natron Valley and the bed of the Bahr-bela-ma) – – – – – | 4 |
| To Muhabag – – – – – – – | 13 |
| Mogara – – – – – – – | 4½ |
| Biljoradeck – – – – – – – | 16 |
| To a station on the hills of Ummesogeir: said to be 40 hours, *or more,* say | 41½ |
| To Ummesogeir – – – – – – – | 5 |
| Siwah – – – – – – – | 20 |
| Total | 123 |

Mr. Browne; but which differs, as has been shewn, only $4\frac{1}{2}$ miles from the other.

It is proper to be remarked, that the people of Siwah, report the distance of Cairo, from that place, to be twelve journies only : but it becomes necessary to inquire what kind of journies these are, in order to turn this, and other reports of the same kind to use. These journies then, are meant for those of light travellers, going few in number together; and not of caravans, where, amongst a number of camels, there must of course be some of slow pace, (to which the whole caravan must, of necessity, conform,) not to mention the increased number of delays by accidents. The people of Siwah reported the length of the following journies, which are in point:

Siwah to Charje, in the Greater Oasis    -    -    12 days.
     Derna    -    -    -    -    -    -    14
     Faiume (through the Lesser Oasis)    -    12
     Cairo    -    -    -    -    -    12

A mean of these, gives about 20,6 per day; the journies to Charje and Faiume giving $19\frac{2}{3}$, the others $21\frac{1}{2}$.* As Siwah lies directly between Derna and the Greater Oasis, we have one line of 26 days, pretty satisfactorily determined in point of distance, and here the result is 20,6 also. Twelve such days would give only 247, of course, for the distance between Cairo and Siwah : so that a rate of $21\frac{1}{2}$ is required. Pliny, lib. v. c. 9, reports twelve journies between Memphis and Ammon, requiring a rate of 21 per day.

There is yet another statement of the distance, and that is, fifteen ordinary *caravan* journies, taken at $16\frac{1}{4}$ or $16\frac{1}{2}$. The result is $247\frac{1}{2}$; about equal to the 12 days of light travelling.

* The ordinary caravan day of 8 hours, appears to be about 20 *British* miles, *by the road;* and in *direct* distance across deserts, about $16\frac{1}{4}$ or $16\frac{1}{2}$ *Geographic* miles.

Possibly, I have taken the distance rather too high, at $259\frac{1}{2}$; but I know not how to do away Mr. Browne's line from the neighbour-hood of Parætonium, considering that Mr. Horneman must have given *his* time from recollection. At all events, Siwah cannot be many miles out, in its longitude; but whilst the longitudes of the places on the sea coast remain in a state of uncertainty, one is not likely to get nearer the truth.

Mr. Browne appears to have been 17 days from his station in lat. 28° 40', and not far to the SW of Siwah, to Alexandria. A rate of $15\frac{1}{3}$ miles is the result; but Mr. Browne being exceedingly ill, the whole way, it is most probable that his attendants relaxed in their speed.

## II. *Siwah to Augila.*

Mr. Horneman's time from Siwah to Augila is $87\frac{1}{2}$ hours,* which, at 2,05 G. miles, give 179,35: but taken on the road distance at $2\frac{1}{2}$ B. miles, as before, $181\frac{1}{4}$. Taken on Horneman's 11 *mean* days, at $16\frac{1}{2}$, it is also $181\frac{1}{2}$. The Arabian geographers reckon it 10 days, implied of 19 G. miles each, equal to 190. Herodotus also allows 10 days between Ammon and Augila.

It is certain, that Mr. Beaufoy's MSS. allow 13 days by the route of Gegabib (the Valley of Dates), which, by Mr. Browne's informa-tion, lies to the NW of Siwah, whilst the ordinary route, by Schiacha,

| | | | | | | | | | |
|---|---|---|---|---|---|---|---|---|---|
| * Siwah to the Valley of *Schiacha* | - | - | - | - | - | | 23 | hours. |
| To Torfaue | - | - | - | - | - | - | - | $6\frac{1}{4}$ | |
| Across the Desert to a watering-place on the border of Augila | | 49 | |
| To Augila | - | - | - | - | - | - | - | - | 9 |
| | | | | | | Total | $87\frac{1}{4}$ | |

leads by the west; but we can hardly suppose that the northern road is two days farther about than the other. Mr. Horneman, it is true, lost his papers at Schiacha, and may not have recollected the exact account of time during the three first days, to that place. I have accordingly allowed 186, as a mean between Mr. Horneman and Edrisi.

Mr. Horneman could not obtain a satisfactory account of the distance between Augila and Bengasi, on the sea coast. Edrisi allows 10 days from Barca; but these, reckoned at 19 each, meet the line from Siwah, in 30° 7', which gives a bearing of W 18° N from the latter; whereas it seems to be the universal opinion, that they lie nearly in the same parallel.*

Delisle and D'Anville go much beyond Edrisi's distance. The latter allows 215 from Barca, which is very probable : and he may perhaps have allowed it from the relations of modern travellers. I have accordingly adopted it; and it meets the line of 186 from Siwah, in lat. 29° 30', lon. 22° 50'. In this position it bears about W ½ N from Siwah.

Ptolemy allows 3° 16' diff. lat. between Derna *(Darnis)* and Augila, which would place the latter, on our Map, in 29½°. He also makes the line of bearing between Ammon and Augila to be nearly parallel to the sea coast, between Parætonium and Derna; and it is certain, although Ptolemy thought otherwise, that the coast lies much to the north of west.

It may be that the longitudes of the places on the coast of Barca,

* Abulfeda and Ptolemy describe it to be so; and Ledyard was told the same at Cairo.

are too far to the west, in M. D'Anville's Maps. Lucas appears to reckon Augila 11 days only, from Bengasi.

### III. *Augila to Fezzan.*

From Augila to Fezzan, Mr. Horneman's time is not kept regularly in hours, the whole way ; owing, perhaps, to the excessive fatigues he underwent in the *Harutsch* or *Black Desert*, in which *whole days* only, are given ; but these were exceedingly long, being usually from morning till night.

All that could be done, was, to reduce these particular days to hours, and add them to the *enumerated* hours in the Journal ; whence there results a total of 195 to 196 hours, at the highest calculation : and these, with proper deductions for the badness of the paths, in the Harutsch, may be taken at 395 G. miles in direct distance.*

---

* This is the computation :

|  | Hours. |
|---|---|
| From Augila to the Mountains of *Moraije* - - - - - | 26 |
| To the Plain of Sultin - - - - - - - - - | 18 |
| Across the Plain or Desert of Sultin, &c. to a woody tract, 3 journies ; but no account in hours, say - - - - - - - - - | 34 |
| To the entrance of the black Harutsch, about 1 day, say - - - | 10 |
| To a watering-place in the Harutsch - - - - - - - | 4 |
| To the end of the black Harutsch, 3½ days ; say - - - - - | 40 |
| Through the white Harutsch, 1½ day ; say - - - - - - | 15 |
| To a watering-place on the borders of Fezzan - - - - | 4 |
| To Temissa - - - - - - - - - - - | 9 |
| Zuila - - - - - - - - - - - - | 6¼ |
| Hamarra - - - - - - - - - - - | 7 |
| Tragan - - - - - - - - - - - | 10¼ |
| Sidi Bisher - - - - - - - - - - | 8 |
| Mourzouk - - - - - - - - - - | 3 |
|  | 195¼ |

The road distance, at 2½ British miles per hour, gives 488¾, which, at ¹⁄₂₀ part for

M. Delisle states the distance at about 405, or 10 more than the above result. He probably collected it from the Journals of modern travellers, as the Arabian geographers allow no less than twenty of their journies between Augila and Zuila, which place is about 60 G. miles short of Mourzouk.

I shall here set forth the reports of divers persons, respecting the distance between Cairo and Fezzan ; which has been taken above, chiefly on the report of Mr. Horneman : and, when reduced to a straight line comes out 829 G. miles.

Messrs. Browne and Ledyard state the distance to be fifty caravan days ; which at 16½, give 825 G. miles.

Edrisi allows forty journies, between Cairo and *Tamest* (Temissa). These, at 19 each, are equal to 760 G. miles : to which, if 73 are added, as Horneman allows, from Temissa to Mourzouk, the total is 833. This route leads through Bahnasa, in the Lesser Oasis ; and, by circumstances, near Siwah also ; as a river occurs at eight days from Bahnasa. Thence it goes to the south of Augila, and by *Seluban*, which may be intended for the Plain of Sultin.*

It is obvious, that if Augila should lie yet more to the south, or nearer in a line between Cairo and Fezzan, this would lengthen the whole line of distance ; and that by 10 or 12 miles.

windings, as before, would give 463¼ ; or in G. miles about 409. I have deducted 14 for the extraordinary windings and roughness of the paths, in the black Harutsch.

Remains G. miles 395, for the direct distance between Augila and Mourzouk.

* Herodotus has a line of distance from Thebes, westward, in intervals of 10 days each, but very inaccurate.

The comparison of the different authorities, then, is as follows

By Horneman, - - - - 829 ⎫
By Browne and Ledyard, - - - 825 ⎭ mean 827
By Edrisi, (direct) - - - - 833
By Edrisi and Abulfeda, reckoned from Siwah
    only, and thence through Augila and Zala 877
By the bearing and distance from Mesurata 854*

Thus Horneman's account falls short of the interval between Cairo and Mourzouk, when the latter is placed in reference to Mesurata, by 25 miles only; and the reported caravan distance falls only four short of Horneman's. The reports of the Arabian geographers ought not to be put in competition with either.

IV. *Respecting the Position of Mourzouk, Capital of Fezzan.*

Mr. Horneman in his Journal transmitted from Tripoly, states the latitude of Mourzouk, by observation, to be $25° 54' 15''$; a parallel so different from the result of the other authorities, that it becomes necessary to examine those authorities, minutely. The reported observation, differs nearly two degrees from the parallel assigned it in the Proceedings of the Association printed in 1798. Without attempting to account for so great an (apparent) error, I shall proceed to adduce the authorities for its parallel, as assumed in the present map.

1. Mr. Beaufoy, from the information of certain Tripoline merchants, has given $17\frac{1}{2}$ journies of the caravan, in a direct south

* The former statement of the distance, (in the Geog. Herod. p. 167.) is 861. The difference is occasioned by the different modes of projection of the maps; that in Herodotus, being on a spherical projection, the present one being rectilinear.

bearing, from Mesurata on the sea coast.* These journies are given at 8 hours, or 20 British miles per day : and I allowed for them 15 geographical miles, in direct distance ; but I shall now, finding by experience that the paths in the Desert are generally very straight, allow 16½ ; whence the 17½ days will be found to produce 288¾, or say 289 G. miles. If these miles were entirely difference of latitude, Mourzouk would not be lower than 27° 22′ 2″, as Mesurata is said to lie in 32° 10′.

2. Another authority adduced by the same gentleman, allows 23 days from Tripoly, by the way of Gwarian and Sockna, which turns out much the same as the former result. The distance from Tripoly to Fezzan, through Mesurata, is 24½ days ; consequently that by Sockna, is the shortest, although now generally disused, on account of its being unsafe.†

The intersection of the two lines of distance from Augila and Mesurata ; that is, 395 G. miles from the former, and 289 from the latter, place Mourzouk in latitude 27° 23′ ; and at 30 G. miles east of the meridian of Mesurata. Consequently, the bearing will be about S. ½ E, instead of south, as reported.

3. Edrisi says, that the distance from *Sort* to Zuila, is nine journies, which, on his scale of 19 per day, are equal to 171 G. miles: and Abulfeda says that they lie N. and S. from each other. Zuila is a point in Horneman's route, about 60 G. miles to the E by N or ENE of Mourzouk : and Sort, according to M. D'Anville, lies in about 30° 28′. Consequently, Zuila, if in the same meridian, should be in

---

* See Proceed. Afr. Assoc. for 1790, chap. iv.

† The road by Sockna, seems to be the *short* road to *Phazania,* mentioned by Pliny, lib. v. c. 5.

latitude 27° 37', or 14 min. to the N. of Mourzouk.   By the construction, Zuila bears about S 7° W from Sort, which, in respect
of the difference of latitude, is much the same thing : and hence,
Mourzouk ought not to be to the south of 27° 23', or thereabouts.

4. Ledyard was told, that Augila lay *west* from Siwah; and
Wadan, (or Zala,) in the way to Fezzan, WSW from Augila.
Horneman gives much the same idea; saying that they went W by S
from Augila, at setting out.   Unfortunately, Mr. Horneman omits
to state the distance between Fezzan and Tripoly, although he
travelled it.

5. *Zala,* (called also *Wadan,**) is said by Edrisi, page 40, to be
nine days SE from Sort; and midway between Augila and Zuila;
that is ten days from both.†   A glance at the map will shew how
utterly improbable it is, that Mourzouk should be below the parallel
of 26°, considering its relative situation to Wadan and Zuila.

Lastly, if it be admitted that Fezzan is the country of the *Garamantes,* (and I know not where else to look for it, according to the
ancient descriptions,) then, its distance from the sea coast, as stated
by Strabo, p. 835, at nine or ten days journey, agrees exactly, if
reckoned to *Garama,* the ancient capital.   Pliny confirms it strongly,
by placing the Garamantes beyond the *Mons Ater,* (of which more,

---

* There are several places of the name of *Wadan,* in this Geography ; the name
designing the conflux of two water-courses, or torrents.   Another Wadan is found
in the road from Mesurata to Fezzan ; and a third, between Fezzan and Bournu.

† Mr. Horneman came, on the day before he entered the black Harutsch, to a
small wood of *green* trees.   This situation accords with that of Zala, being just midway between Augla and Zuila.   No town is known to exist there, at present.

under the article *Harutsch,*) which will be proved clearly to mean the rocky Desert of *Souda,* between Fezzan and Mesurata.

It should be remarked, that this alteration in the position of Mourzouk, which is about 39 miles to the SE of its position in the map of 1798, does not, in any material degree, affect the interval of space between it and Tombuctoo.*

* M. D'Anville reckons the distance between Tripoly and Mourzouk 240 G. miles, only: M. Delisle about 280, or less: and Sanuto, who wrote on the African Geography, (A. D. 1588,) 255. Thus, the 289 allowed above, from Mesurata, go beyond the highest calculation hitherto made, from Tripoly, which is yet farther from Mourzouk, than Mesurata is.

# CHAPTER II.

General Remarks on the Countries, in the Line of Mr. Horneman's Route.

I SHALL next proceed to offer some geographical, and other, remarks, on certain of the subjects that present themselves in and about the line of Mr. Horneman's route; as, 1. The *Bahr-bela-ma*, and *Valley* of *Mogara*. 2. *Siwah*. 3. The *Lesser Oasis*. 4. The *Valleys* of *Schiacha* and *Gegabib*. 5. *Augila*. 6. The *Harutsch*. 7. *Fezzan* and *Gadamis*.

I. *The Bahr-bela-ma, and Valley of Mogara.*

The term *Bahr* is well known to signify (in Arabic) an expanse of water, whether *sea, lake,* or *river :* and *Bahr-bela-ma,* a hollow space that is supposed to have contained them : in other words, the sea, lake, or river, *without water.* In its application to the present subject, it has been understood by some great authorities, to be the ancient bed of a river; and that river, the Nile of Egypt; which they suppose to have quitted its present course, at Benjusef, and, passing through the province of Faiume, and the lake Kairun, entered the sea at the Gulf of the Arabs. Having already given an opinion on this subject, I shall say no more concerning it in this place, than that it is by no means weakened by any thing that has appeared since : that opinion was, " that in *ancient times* the bed of the

Nile lay lower than the province of Faiume:" and it is certain, that the gap, or outlet at Sakkara, is *still* above the level of the Nile.

Mr. Horneman's observations, added to those of General Andreossy, and of Mr. Browne, throw some further light on the course of the *hollow* bed, or channel in question.

It appears that the General, as well as Mr. Browne,* came to the Natron Valley at about 32 G. miles to the westward of Terané: and that the General also found, adjacent to it, on the west, separated only by a narrow ridge, a second and larger valley, which the Arabs name *Bahr-bela-ma;* and also *Bahr-el-farigh,* which signifies the *empty* river. These he found to run parallel to each.other, in a direction of about NNW $\frac{1}{2}$ W and SSE $\frac{1}{2}$ E, for about 30 miles; and without any appearance of termination, either way. The Natron Valley, he reckons $2\frac{1}{2}$ French leagues, or about $6\frac{1}{2}$ G. miles, in breadth; the other, 3 leagues, or $7\frac{3}{4}$ such miles; or, both together, from one extreme to the other, more than $14\frac{1}{4}$. See the *Mémoires,* p. 239, 240, and also the map.

Mr. Horneman, in his way westward from Cairo, passed the Natron Valley, at the distance of about 40 G. miles from Cairo; and, by circumstances, not more than 9 or 10 from the extreme southern part seen by General Andreossy. At the distance of about 8 miles from the Natron Valley he *descended*, and came to what he calls the foot of a *sand hill;* but it being *dark*, he could not form

---

* Mr. Browne, who did *not* see the Bahr-bela-ma, was *told* that it lay a day's journey to the west of the Natron Lakes; but unless it takes a turn to the west, beyond the point where General A. saw it, he must have been misinformed. See an account of the Bahr-bela-ma in the province of Faiume, in the Geog. Herod. p. 503. The description of these valleys is to be found in the *Mémoires sur l'Egypte,* p. 212.

any idea of the place itself, or of the adjacent country : he however observes, that it will be proper for future travellers to look in this place, for the *course* of the *Bahr-bela-ma* : doubtless, because he found a deep and capacious hollow ; but concerning which, he gives no farther intimation. Adverting, therefore, to the description of General Andreossy, I regard the *sand hill* rather as the *ridge* that separates the two valleys or hollows, than as the thing Mr. Horneman took it for. He says, that they *descended* the sand hill, in *indescribable* disorder;* which seems to imply a *long*, as well as a *steep* descent: and, leaving the place, before it was light enough to form a judgment of the nature of it, he only directs the attention of others to it: surely, because it was a hollow tract.

It may be allowed, therefore, that the Bahr-bela-ma and Natron Valleys extend 40 or more G. miles, pointing northward to the Lake Mareotis, or to the Gulf of the Arabs; and on the other hand, towards the quarter of the lake of Kairun ; from whence they seem to be less than 30 miles distant.

The four hours of travelling, between the station at the Natron Valley, and the foot of the sand hill, does not ill agree with the ground. The breadth of the Natron Valley, $6\frac{1}{2}$ G. miles, is, reckoning the ascent on the west, equal to $3\frac{1}{4}$ hours travelling ; and General Andreossy says, that he was 40 minutes in descending the slope, to the bottom of the Bahr-bela-ma. (Mem. p. 240.) Here then we have made out nearly the four hours : besides, it is not certain that the hollows may not have been crossed obliquely, by Mr. Horneman.

It appears that M. D'Anville believed the existence of, and has expressed on his map of Egypt, a hollow or valley, extending the

* This (I am given to understand) is the idea conveyed in the original Journal.

whole way from the lake Kairun, to the neighbourhood of the Gulf of the Arabs. The French, it seems, have never had an opportunity of determining the questions ; which appears extraordinary. I shall now proceed to the description of another valley, which may possibly be a branch of the Bahr-bela-ma.

### Valley of Mogara.

Mr. Horneman states, that the morning on which he left the *foot of the sand hill,* he entered the Desert which may be considered as " the natural limit of Egypt." This Desert extends more than 150 G. miles from east to west : its extent southward, is not known, but it probably borders on the Lesser Oasis. Whether it be a part of that great sandy desert of twelve journies across, between the Greater Oasis and Siwah, Mr. Horneman had no opportunity of knowing ; as he remained in uncertainty respecting the course of the *Ummesogeir* hills, southward.

This Desert, perfectly flat, and covered with shifting sand, is bounded northward by a chain of bare calcareous hills, running nearly east and west, in the line of our traveller's route. On the side towards the Desert, they are steep, and are bordered by a re-markable valley or hollow, known to extend from the *neighbourhood* of the Bahr-bela-ma, to the length of a journey of seven days westward. Its breadth is from one mile, to six; it had much standing water in it, at certain seasons ; but when Mr. Horneman saw it (in September 1798,) it had only some small lakes or ponds, at intervals; and in several places, tracts of marshy or swampy land, extending for several miles together. The water of the pools was bitter ; but sweet water was found close to them, on digging to the depth of four to six feet. (See above, p. 10.) The caravans in this route, keep along the edge of the valley, availing themselves of its resources of water, every two or three days; but preferring the sandy path, as being best adapted to the feet of the camels.

How far the valley extends westwards, is not known to us : whether it terminates at the place where Mr. Horneman ascended the hills of Ummesogeir, (which form a continuation of the range of calcareous hills before-mentioned;) or whether it communicates with those valleys, which contain the Greater or Lesser Oasis. Be it as it will, it seems to partake of the nature of those valleys ; being situated at the foot of steep calcareous hills, and below the level of the flat Desert beneath them. It is remarked, that the steep sides of all these ranges face the south or west.* In one particular, however, this valley of Mogara, differs very widely from those which contain the Oasis, (although it seems very much akin to that of *Schiacha ;* of which more in the sequel,) in that no water springs up to the surface ; to which cause we may probably attribute the absence of such tracts of land, as are denominatd *Oases.* The springs indeed, appear to me, to be a characteristic feature of the Oases.

We learn a curious particular from General Andreossy, whilst speaking of the Bahr-bela-ma. He says, (Mém. sur l'Egypte, p. 246,) that the people of Terané on the Nile, transport from a valley situated three days journey beyond the Bahr-bela-ma, a species of *rushes,* which are manufactured into mats at Menouf, in the Delta. The General supposes the place in question to be a continuation of the Bahr-bela-ma, into the interior of Africa ; and indeed it may well be, that the valley of Mogara is a branch of the former ; separating from it, at, or near, the place where Mr. Horneman

* The hills over the valley of Mogara, answer to the hills of *Le Magra*, (perhaps corrupted from *El Mogara*,) of Mr. Beaufoy ; Afr. Assoc. 1790, ch. x. and also to the M. *Ogdamus* of Ptolemy, Afr. Tab. III.

crossed it. The place alluded to by the General, may be about *Biljoradek*, and in one of the swampy tracts spoken of above : or if the three journies are meant from *Terané*, as is not impossible, that it will be about *Mogara*. At all events, we must regard this valley as the place intended by General Andreossy.

This gentleman's description of the Bahr-bela-ma is well worthy of attention, but is too long to be inserted here. He found in it, petrified wood, of the same kind with that seen by Horneman, in the adjacent sandy Desert : * but both of them remark, that the wood has not any mark of a tool on it, as some have fancifully imagined, and have thence regarded the valley as an ancient bed of the Nile, deserted about the date of the foundation of Memphis.

No doubt the hollow in question very much resembles a water-course, both as to form, and from its having pebbles in it ; but where is the body of fresh water that could have scooped it out, or have filled it ? General Andreossy reckons it nearly nine British miles in breadth, and exceedingly deep; and the Nile does not at any time carry a body of water, equal to one mile in breadth ! What the state of things was, at an earlier period of the world, we know not, but within the reach of history, the Nile appears to have been much of the same bulk, as at present.

But this is not the only difficulty. The province of Faiume, through which the supposed issue of the Nile must have been, is separated from the valley of the Nile, by a continuation of the ridge of hills that forms the western wall of Egypt; and through which, (if I understand the matter right,) the passage to the lake of Kairun, by *Illabon* and *Hawara*, has been made by art. At all events, this

* See above, p. 8.

canal or passage cannot be regarded as the continuation of the ancient bed of the Nile from *Upper Egypt* into the *Bahr-bela-ma*, because of its confined dimensions : and of course, all idea of the Nile having detached a *western branch*, or thrown itself into the bed of the lake of Kairun and Bahr-bela-ma, is done away ; for even admitting the continuity of these, the hollow that contains the lake, and also constitutes the province of Faiume, must be regarded as a kind of *cul de sac* to the Bahr-bela-ma, whilst the hills by Illahon existed. And hence I took occasion to remark, elsewhere,\* that it is possible, that the famous work of the lake Moeris, which now forms a kind of enigma amongst the learned, might have been formed by the very act of cutting through a low part of the western wall of Egypt, and letting the water into the hollow space which now contains the lake of Kairun. But had the Nile ever formed its alluvions adjacent to the Gulf of the Arabs, there would surely be some traces of them remaining, either along the shore, or ·in the sea itself.

It may be remarked, that there are other valleys or hollows along the course of the Nile, almost equally extensive with that of Faiume, but to whose level the Nile is not *yet* risen. And here it may not be out of the way to repeat what has been said in another place,† that although the Nile in these times, when swoln, flows into the lake Kairun, yet there must have been a time, when its bed was too low to reach it : for it cannot be doubted, that its bed has been gradually rising, by deposition ; a necessary effect of the protrusion of the lands of the Delta into the sea : and, of course, that it *will continue* to rise. ‡

* In the Geogr. of Herod. p. 504. † *Ibid.*

‡ This is explained in the observations on the alluvions of rivers, in the same book, Section xviii.

The progress of the moving sands of Lybia, eastward, into the Bahr-bela-ma, &c. is treated of by General Andreossy, Mem. page 247, and is also well worthy of attention. This movement appears to take place, very generally ; and Mr. Horneman remarks, that in their line of course, every obstruction gives rise to a sand hill ; but he more particularly remarks a smaller kind of sand hill, formed by the obstruction of the trunks of palm trees ; and so high as to leave to the view, nothing more than the topmost branches.

## II. *Siwah.*

The geographical position of this remarkable place, considered generally, cannot now be questioned; since we possess, in addition to the information communicated by Mr. Browne, that of Mr. Horneman ; both in respect of the time employed on his way thither, and of the reports of the natives, concerning its relative position to Cairo, the Oases, Faiume, and Derna : and when it is considered that these new authorities differ from the former ones, by a few minutes of longitude only.

The report of Mr. Horneman is no less favourable to the former idea, of its being the OASIS of AMMON ; and the remains of the Egyptian structure within it, those of the famed Temple of Jupiter Ammon : the honour of which original discovery is due to Mr. Browne. For, in addition to what may be deemed the *inner* temple, Mr. Horneman has viewed the foundations indicated by Mr. Browne, in circumference some hundred paces; and even some remains of the walls themselves, of what may be supposed to have been the *including* temple; the materials of which are probably existing in the construction of the stone houses of a town, estimated to contain

a population of six to seven thousand\* persons. We need no longer
to entertain a doubt, founded on the disappearance of the materials
of the temple and palace described by the ancients. Besides, on a
review of the subject, so many particulars accord with the ancient
descriptions; such as the dimensions, and accordance of geographical situation; the fruits, the copious fountains, fertility of soil; and
finally, although a negative proof, perhaps one of the strongest circumstances of all, the declaration of the inhabitants, that " no other
fertile spot exists in the vicinity; or nearer than the Lesser Oasis."

A proof of the populousness and affluence of the ancient state of
Ammon, exists in the numerous catacombs pointed out to, or visited
by, Browne and Horneman: and by the probability that the rocky
hill on which the modern town stands, is also full of catacombs.
Such are indeed known to exist within the habitations of the people
of the neighbouring village of Ummesogeir; which may thence be
supposed, notwithstanding its present miserable state, to have been
a flourishing appendage to ancient Ammon: and might probably
have been the *Siropum* of Ptolemy.

One particular requires discussion. Mr. Horneman differs very
widely from Mr. Browne, in his estimation of the extent of the territory of Siwah. Mr. Browne reckons it six miles by four: but
Mr. Horneman a *circumference* of 50 miles. His words are, " a
well-watered valley of 50 miles in circuit, surrounded by naked
steep rocks." (Abulfeda also says, that the territory is environed

---

\* My friend, Mr. Morton Pitt, M. P. has proved, by the enumeration of the inhabitants of a country parish in Dorsetshire, that the men of an age *capable* of bearing
arms are *one-fourth* of the whole community. Mr. Horneman, if I understand him
rightly, states the number of *actual* warriors to be 1500 ; so that we ought, perhaps,
to multiply that number by 5, to get nearer to the total amount of the population.

by hills.)  Very probably, Mr. Horneman's idea goes to the whole
space inclosed by the hills; Mr. Browne's to the fertile part of it
only; and it must be acknowledged, that the dimensions given by
the latter, accord with those of the ancients.

Mr. Horneman says, that *all* the waters of the springs, are con-
sumed in the irrigation of the gardens and fields; so that no stream
flows *beyond* the district.  It is certain, that Edrisi describes a *river*
named *Costara*, at eight journies from Bahnasa, in the Lesser Oasis,
towards Fezzan; agreeing almost exactly with the distance to Siwah
from Cairo, fifteen days; which, at 19 G. miles, are equal to 285;
and the construction has 275. According to Mr. Horneman's description of the copious and numerous springs in Siwah, one of which
alone, he says, forms a considerable rivulet, and another, several
rivulets, it might be expected that some of the waters flowed to a
considerable distance before they were entirely absorbed in the
sands.  The Costara river, may, however, flow from a distinct fountain in the Desert: but the coincidence of position is remarkable.

The description of the lands of Siwah, by Mr. Horneman, and of
the Greater Oasis, by Mr. Browne, appear to be of the same nature;
each possessing copious fountains and verdant fields, fitted either for
pasture or cultivation.  The lands of the Lesser Oasis are said to
be much the same, though rather inferior: whence it would seem,
that the Valley of Mogara, which has good water at the depth of
four feet, only wants that it should spring up to the surface, in
order to form it into an Oasis, like the others!

## III. *The Lesser Oasis.*

Mr. Horneman was told that at the distance of seven journies from Siwah, five from Faiume, and at only a *few* from Biljoradek, there existed a country, similar to Siwah, and whose inhabitants, who are less numerous, spoke the *same language*. He with reason, concluded it to be a part of the Lesser Oasis of the ancients; and, from its position, it ought to be the northern extremity.

If by a few days journey, when five and seven have been mentioned before, we may understand three, or thereabouts, the place in question, should lie in the parallel of 28° 50′; at about midway between Cairo and Siwah;* and 89 G. miles to the westward of Bahnasa, at the canal of Joseph. Hence it falls very near to Bahnasa, in the Oasis, which has been already placed,† at 83 from the forementioned place.

Ptolemy places the Lesser Oasis in lat 28° 45′: and at 75 G. miles to the west of *Oxyrinchus*, taken for the last mentioned Bahnasa. He no doubt meant to express some particular point in the Oasis; and that point, probably, the principal town, which may have been on the site of Bahnasa in the Oasis. So that there is a general agreement between the ancient and the modern accounts of it.‡

But Mr. Browne, when at Charje in the Greater Oasis, was told, that the southern part of the Lesser Oasis, named by the inhabitants

---

* Edrisi places it at seven journies from Cairo ; probably through Faiume.
† Geography of Herodot. p. 560, 561.
‡ Most of the modern authors, who have mentioned this Oasis, speak of *ruins* existing in it. In particular Mr. Browne, p. 133.

*Al-wah-el-Gherbi*, was only forty miles distant to the northward. This being the case, the Lesser Oasis should have an extent of more than 100 miles from north to south : that is, more than the other tract, of the same name, denominated the *Greater*; but which may, nevertheless, be true, as the term greater or lesser, may refer to other qualities than dimensions. Mr. Browne describes the Greater Oasis (which he had traversed throughout) to consist of large detached spots or islands, like Siwah, extending in a chain from N to S, and separated by intervals of desert from two to fourteen hours of travelling. The Lesser Oasis, most probably, is much of the same nature; but is, by general report, inferior to the other, and vastly inferior to Siwah. See an account of the Oases in the Geog of Herodotus, Sections xx. and xxi.

Mr. Browne adds, that the Lesser Oasis is a kind of capital settlement of the Muggrebine (or western) Arabs, who pass from it, to the western extremity of the lake Kairun; whose shore, on that side, is also in their possession. (Pages 132, 170.)

Thus, our modern travellers have fixed, pretty satisfactorily, in the view of general geography, the positions of all the three Oases : but it would be more satisfactory to have correctly the latitude of the northern extremity of the Lesser one, as well as some account of the number and position of the *islands* contained in it.

## IV. *Valleys of Schiacha, and Gegabib.*

At the distance of about three days journey to the westward of Siwah, Mr. Horneman came to *Schiacha*, a *fruitful* valley on the right; and, as appears from a circumstance that occurred during the unpleasant visit of the Siwahans, there were many little *bogs*, in the neighbourhood of their camp, in that valley. Again, at six hours farther, was *Torfaue*, where they also obtained fresh water. Moreover, in the way from Siwah to Schiacha, at the distance of 6 or 7 miles from the former, he saw at the foot of the hills, a lake, implied to be of fresh water, (see Journal, page 57,) of several miles in extent.

Combining with this, the remark of Mr. Horneman, that they had travelled by a chain of hills from Siwah; that these hills were a continuation of those which they had always seen to the *northward* of their route through the Desert; and that they " rose immediately from the level ground of the Desert, without any declivity, and without any arenacious, or other cover, only the bare rock being seen;" one may conclude, that the valley described, at the foot of these hills, is much of the same nature, with that of *Mogara*. Moreover, it appears, that he considered the whole extent of the hills, from the Bahr-bela-ma *to* Schiacha, at least, as one continued ridge; and which has an abrupt declivity to the south. The *continuity*, however, remains to be proved.

The remarkable valley of *Gegabib*, famous for its dates, cannot be far from the neighbourhood of *Schiacha* and *Torfaue*; since Mr. Browne says, page 26, that when he had advanced two journies to the north-westward of Siwah, he was *not far* from Gegabib. Mr. Beaufoy calls it, from the description of Ben Ali, " a narrow plain, sandy, and uninhabited, but fertile in dates;" which, he adds, are gathered by the people of *Duna* on the sea coast, eight journies distant.* As Mr. Horneman remarked no date trees on his way

* (See Proceed. Afr. Assoc. 1790, ch. x.) The sea coast is truly about eight journies from Gegabib: but I know of no place of the name of *Duna*. Derna is twice that distance.

from Siwah to Augila, his route must have been wide of this valley
or plain, and no doubt to the *south* of it. This seems proved by
Ben Ali's description of the route from Augila to Siwah, which lay
" *across* the extensive *mountains* of *Gerdoba,*" to this valley; since
Mr. Horneman left the mountains to the northward of him, the
whole way.

As the dates of Gegabib are now gathered by the people of the
sea coast; and those of Augila in ancient times, by the *Nasamones*
of the coast of the *Syrtis;* so the people of the *same* coast, aided
by the modern *Augilans,* undertake expeditions ten days journey
inland from *Augila,* to *steal* men and dates, at present!* So that
this system of inroad, from the quarter towards the coast, inland,
seems to have been practised at all times; and I shall have occasion
to remark it again, hereafter. Augila was an inhabited place in the
time of Herodotus, and yet the dates were carried off by strangers:
and it seems the present Augilans retaliate on others, the injuries
sustained by their ancestors.

## V. *Augila.*

This small, but celebrated territory, is situated nearly midway
between Egypt and Fezzan; and somewhat less than 170 miles
from the nearest coast of the Mediterranean. It seems to possess
much of the character of an Oasis, being flat, well watered, fertile,
and surrounded by arid deserts, either sandy or rocky; in particular, that to the west is so destitute of herbage, that the camels of
Mr. Horneman's caravan, carried their provender with them. Its
extent from east and west, seems to be little more than a long
day's journey. The agriculture of the Augilans is confined more to

* See above, page 108.

gardening, than to raising of corn : but Mr. Horneman is silent respecting the culture of dates, for which it has been so celebrated
both in ancient and modern times. *

It appears that the Augilans are the merchants who carry on the
commerce between Egypt and Fezzan; for which, their middle situation, and ready communication with the port of Bengasi, qualify them.
The people of one of their most populous towns, † *Mojabra*, are
solely occupied with this commerce : and Mr. Horneman contrasts,
in a most unfavourable light, the character of these traders, with
the people of the other towns, whose employment is agriculture. In
a few short remarks, we are shewn, in the most pointed manner, the
natural, and almost necessary effect, of the occupations of mankind
on their moral habits. Notwithstanding the possession of this commerce, Augila is still a very poor place indeed.

It may be remarked, that *Augila* is one of the few places in Africa
that has preserved its ancient name entire.

## VI. *The Harutsch, White and Black.*

These remarkable tracts (of which see the description above,
page 48 *et seq.*) had been noticed by Ben Ali, to Mr. Beaufoy, who
has recorded them (in chap. x. of the Proceed. Afr. Assoc. for 1790;)
the one under the description of the rocky Desert of *black* and *naked*

---

* Abulfeda speaks both of its dates and its fountains : and Ben Ali informed Mr.
Beaufoy, that it was famous for the " *abundance* and *flavour*" of its dates. Proceed.
Afr. Assoc. ch. x.

† Mr. Horneman speaks of three towns in Augila, and Ben Ali adds a fourth town,
or village, *Guizara*, situated at one journey to the east of the capital. Hence it agrees
with the watering-place to which Mr. Horneman came at nine hours short of Augila.
It seems to be also the *Saragma* of Ptolemy. (Tab. III. Africæ.)

*rock*, of four days extant ; the other, of *soft* and *sandy* stone, of three days extent : but they are described in a very obscure manner, and their respective positions are transposed.

Mr. Horneman appears to have employed nearly fifty hours in crossing the *black* Harutsch ; fourteen more in the *white* Harutsch ; or altogether sixty-four hours, equal to eight ordinary caravan days; which does not differ very widely from the report of Ben Ali, who allowed *seven*.

The white Harutsch forms the extreme boundary of Fezzan, and extends southward, into the district of the *Tibbo Rshade ;* of which more in the sequel. The black Harutsch appears to be much more extensive. Horneman was told, that it was in breadth five journies from east to west; (he crossed it in WSW direction ;) and in length seven, from north to south. However, Mr. Horneman justly observes, that it must be more extensive, since he crossed a tract of the same nature, in his way from Fezzan to Tripoly; and even from that point it was said to extend a considerable distance to the west. He adds, that he learnt at Mourzouk, that there were black mountains also in the road from that place to Bornou : that is, to the south-east.

Mr. Beaufoy was also informed, (See chap. iv. Afr. Proceed. 1790,) that a desert named *Souda,* (that is, *black,*) is crossed in the way from Mesurata to Fezzan; agreeing with Mr. Horneman's report. The breadth, in a north and south direction, is given at four days, or somewhat narrower than in Mr. Horneman's line of route from Augila.

Mr. Horneman describes the black Harutsch to consist of matter,

that, in his idea, was volcanic, or had undergone the action of fire :
and its conformation appears very singular indeed.  There exists in
Pliny, an evident proof that it was known to the Romans ; for they
had crossed it, in their expeditions to Fezzan, and towards the
Niger, &c. ; and had even explored and remarked the shortest route
across the same mountains.

Pliny says, that " from *Cydamus* (i. e. *Gadamis*, which, by the
bye, he says lies opposite to *Sabrata,* on the sea coast) there extends
a mountain a long way to the east, called by the Romans, MONS
ATER ; and which appears as if it were burnt or scorched by the
rays of the sun." (Lib. v. c. 5.)  And he adds, that beyond those
mountains, are deserts, and the towns of the Garamantes, which
were conquered by the Romans under Balbus.  In this description,
we clearly recognise the SOUDA, or BLACK DESERT, to the north of
Fezzan ; and which Mr. Horneman *saw,* both there, and to the
east, of the same country; and also *learnt,* that it *continued* far westward, beyond the line of the road from Fezzan to Mesurata : in
other words, towards Gadamis.

Sockna, which is a town of some consideration, lies midway between this road and Gadamis : and it is known that the Desert of
*Souda* passes to the south of it.  So that there is little doubt but
that Pliny is right, in extending the *Mons Ater* westward to *Cydamus,* (*i. e.* Gadamis) and to a long extent eastward of it.

## VII. *Fezzan.*

It has been said, that there is no material difference between the
position of the capital of this country (Mourzouk), as given by Mr.
Horneman, and the former assumed position in the maps, drawn

for the African Association, in 1790 and 1798; considered in the view of general geography. It is for this reason, that I have not altered it in the general Map, but have accommodated the positions eastward to it; instead of altering the entire Map. But in the Map of Mr. Horneman's Route, all the positions affected by his observations, are given according to those observations.

Neither do the boundaries and extent, as given by Mr. Horneman, differ materially from those given by Mr. Beaufoy; which is remarkable, considering under what disadvantage he collected his materials, compared with the mode of collecting them on the spot. But in arranging the boundaries, a distinction is to be made between the *proper* country of Fezzan, and its *dependencies*.

Mr. Horneman says, that the *cultivated* part of Fezzan has an extent of 300 British miles from north to south; by 200 from east to west: which dimensions have a general agreement with Mr. Beaufoy's, in respect of the *area* of *the whole;* but Mr. Beaufoy makes it a circle, whilst Mr. Horneman makes it an oval. It would appear, also, that Mr. Horneman reckons the whole extent thus given by himself and Mr. Beaufoy as cultivated land; and we know too little of the actual geography to attempt any detail. Mr. Horneman came to the eastern border of Fezzan at 44 to 45 hours, equal to about 110 B. miles by the road, from Mourzouk. In order to justify Mr. Horneman's calculation, Mourzouk ought to stand nearly in the centre, between the eastern and western limits; but Mr. Beaufoy says, that the territory does not extend far to the west of the capital.

Again, Mr. Beaufoy allows five days from the northern boundary, at the edge of the black Desert, to Mourzouk: that is, about

100 B. miles by the road.  And from Mourzouk southward to the mountains of *Eyre*, the southern boundary, fourteen days ; equal to 280 such miles : total 380 : or perhaps, in direct distance, 350 such miles.  But there lies in the midway, a desert of five journies in breadth ; and it is uncertain to what point Mr. Horneman reckons.

The dependencies are very extensive.  The regions of the Harutsch, together with Wadan, Houn, (or Hun), and Sockna, all of which lie *beyond* the Harutsch, Mr. Horneman classes as belonging to Fezzan.  Sockna should be a place of note, as its merchants are in possession of the chief part of the commerce, between Fezzan and Tripoly.

Mr. Horneman was informed that there are 101 inhabited *places* in Fezzan ; and it is remarkable that this is precisely the number stated in M. Delisle's Map of Africa, drawn in 1707 ; and Mr. Beaufoy's informant said, little less than 100.  But amongst these, there are few places of note, and still fewer whose positions are given ; and in the report of these, Mr. Beaufoy's informant differs in some respect, from Mr. Horneman.

Of the position of the capital, Mourzouk, I have already spoken, very fully.

Zuila, or Zawila, (probably the *Cillaba* of Pliny, lib. v. c. 5.) is placed, by Mr. Horneman's route, at 59 G. miles to the *eastward* of Mourzouk.  Mr. Beaufoy was told that it was 7 days journey distant, and the bearing, in his reports, varies from *east* to *ENE*.  I have allowed E by N.  This was the capital in the time of Edrisi : *

* Mr. Horneman saw some remains, which ought to be referred to the time of Mahomedanism.

and probably, from this circumstance, some of the neighbouring nations still call the country of Fezzan, *Seela*, as we are told by Mr. Horneman.

Temissa, another principal town, is placed by Mr. Horneman about 7 hours travelling, to the eastward of Zuila. This appears to be the *Tamest* of Edrisi, situated at 40 journies (of his scale) from Cairo.

Germa, or Jermah, is placed, by Mr. Beaufoy, *southward* from Zuila, and at nearly the same distance from Mourzouk. This is unquestionably the *Garama* of the Romans,* the capital of Fezzan, or *Phazania*, at the time of the Roman conquest; and which appears to have given the name of *Garamantes* to the whole nation. (As the discussion of this subject is already before the Public, in the Geography of Herodotus, Section XXII. the Author begs leave to refer to it). Mr. Horneman, who names this place *Yerma*, places it to the *west* of the capital : however, M. D'Anville has placed it under the name of *Gherma*, to the SE, with *Tessoua* (or Tosaûa) between the two; and this is Mr. Beaufoy's arrangement of it. It should be noticed that M. D'Anville places these towns out of all proportion too far to the south-east of Mourzouk ; being unconscious that *Gherma*, or *Garama*, was situated within Fezzan, although he recognises it as the capital of the *Garamantes*.

Kattron is placed SE from the capital, by Mr. Beaufoy, distant 60 road miles. This is the *Gatron* of Mr. Horneman, placed by him directly south. D'Anville names it *Catron*, and places it about

---

* There are considerable remains of structures, at this day. See Proceed. Afr. Assoc. 1790, chap. iv.

SSW, distant 75 G. miles. In another place, where Mr. Horneman describes a march of troops from Fezzan to Burgu, he reckons Gatron S 54 miles from Mourzouk, in the way to Teghery; which being, by every account, to the west of south, from Mourzouk, it may be inferred that Katron lies to the southward, rather than to the south-eastward. The report of the distance differs but little between Mr. Horneman and Mr. Beaufoy. M. D'Anville probably was not so well informed as either of these gentlemen, in respect of the distance.

Mendra is said, by Mr. Beaufoy, to be 60 miles nearly south, from the capital. But this is the position of Katron, according to Horneman, and which, as we have seen, appears probable: and Mendra being a *province*, as well as a town, must be in some other situation. Possibly, it ought to change places with Katron, in Mr. Beaufoy's description.

Teghery is given by Mr. Beaufoy, as the most westerly, or rather south-westerly town of Fezzan; and he places it SW 80 road miles from the capital. The same place appears in a route (mentioned before) from Mourzouk to Burgu, by Mr. Horneman, who places it SSW 33 such miles, from Katron; whence the position of Teg-hery would be about S $\frac{3}{4}$ W, 85 miles. But D'Anville places it at SSW $\frac{1}{2}$ W 116 G. miles from Mourzouk; and although the distance in this case, as in that of Katron, is excessive, yet some regard ought to be had to the bearing. Accordingly, a mean of the three gives S 26 W; and the mean distance of Beaufoy and Horneman 68 G. miles, reduced to a direct line.

A place named Tai-garee appears in a route from Tunis to Kashna, communicated by Mr. Magrah, at fifteen journies from

Gadamis.* It appears highly probable that this is the same place
with Teghery in Fezzan: but the distance arising on the fifteen
journies falls very short of the position of Teghery, placed as above.
Could this point be ascertained, it would operate as a check on the
position of Mourzouk; and I cannot but suspect, that this capital
is somewhat more to the west, or north-west, than it now stands
in the Map.

These facts are particularly noticed here, that future geographers
may inquire, whether the route of the Tunis caravan, to Soudan,
passes through Teghery in the western skirt of the country of
Fezzan; as I conceive it doth: and also that there is some error in
the combination of the geographical context, between Tunis, and
the eastern positions, which prevents the closing of the lines, to
the aforesaid town of Teghery.

One cannot dismiss the subject of Fezzan, without remarking,

* Gadamis, it would appear, ought to be placed more to the eastward than it appears in the Map of 1798; which will increase the direct distance of Teghery from
Tunis, on the Map, by straightening the line of the road.

Gadamis was pointed out to Mr. Magrah, to bear from Tunis, S 4° E; the distance 23 caravan days. Of these, the first 10 were to Kabes, situated in the Map of
D'Anville at 163½ G. miles, in a direction of S a very little W from Tunis. If the
other 13 days (at the same rate of 16,35) equal to 212½ G. miles, be laid off on the
line of S 4 E from Tunis, Gadamis will fall in latitude 30° 29′ 30″, longitude 11°
east.

Mr. Magrah was told that it bore SW from Tripoly, but no distance is given.
Pliny says, that *Cydamus* lies opposite to *Sabrata* (Sabart, or old Tripoly). In one
copy of Pliny, it is reckoned 12 journies from the Greater Syrtis. In this position it
is somewhat more than 240 G. miles from it; agreeing to 12 journies of the rate of
*light* travelling, described above, page 126.

These *data* may be of use in the future corrections of the geography, as Gadamis
may, from its position, be a useful point of outset.

that the observations of Mr. Horneman have added another proof of its being the country intended by the ancient authors, for that of the Garamantes. For he has shewn us, that the black rocky Desert, the continuation of the *black Harutsch,* passes between Fezzan and Tripoly, and extends yet farther west, towards Gadamis; and as Pliny places the *Mons Ater* in this position, with a desert and the cities of the *Garamantes* beyond them, these cities cannot well be any others than those of Fezzan. (See above, page 151). I shall also mention, in its place, another circumstance brought to light by Mr. Horneman, concerning the *Troglodytæ* mentioned by Herodotus, in the neighbourhood of the Garamantes; and which induces a very strong belief that the people bordering on the south-east of Fezzan, are meant.

# CHAPTER III.

*Improvements in the general Geography of North Africa.—Remote Sources of the Nile, and Termination of the Niger.—Lake of Fittré, or Kauga.*

THIS division of the present subject respects the improvements of the general geography of the eastern quarter of North Africa. Since the construction of the General Map, in 1798,* much new matter has appeared in the Travels of Mr. Browne: and to these are now to be added, the observations and inquiries of Mr. Horneman. These important notices will be found mutually to explain and confirm each other, as far as they go, over the same ground; and which is to a very considerable extent.

Mr. Browne has the advantage in point of materials proper for mathematical geography; whilst Mr. Horneman's range of inquiry, though equally extended, consists more of general notices, in the nature of sketches. Both possess very great merit; both appear indefatigable in collecting the most useful matter that either presented itself, or could be procured: and how much soever a person at his ease, and in a state of perfect security, may blame the want of a clear and connected series of notices, respecting the geography and present state of the countries treated of; yet it should be considered,

---

* That Map has been corrected accordingly ; and is placed opposite.

been expected. The same may be said of Sennaar, in respect of Darfoor; Mr. Browne being satisfied, that the interval of distance between them, agreed to the observations; the one being determined by Mr. Bruce, the other by himself. Mr. D'Anville had placed Sennaar nearly four degrees of longitude too far to the west, in his map of Africa, 1749.*

It may be observed, that between Egypt and Darfoor, no waters whatsoever communicate with the Nile, from the west: and that Mr. Browne was assured, that the same state of things existed to the south, between Darfoor and the head of the White River. So far indeed, from any water running to the east in that quarter, he was told (and the fact is corroborated in part by others,) that the waters to the west and south-west of Darfoor, all ran to the *west* or *north-west*.

Mr. Browne relates, from the information of the people at Darfoor, that the head of the White River consists of a number of streams, issuing from certain lofty mountains named *Kumri*, or *Komri*, situated in a country named *Donga*, distant a month's journey from Shilluk; which is itself 3¼ days short of Sennaar: so that the *remotest* spring of the White River may be 45 journies from Sennaar. Now, some of the slaves brought in the Darfoorian caravan to Cairo, told Mr. Ledyard that they came from a place 55.

* Mr. Bruce describes a chain of mountains, extending westward from the Abyssynian branch of the Nile, between the 11th and 12th degree of north latitude; and having to the north *Dyre* and *Tegla*. As these places are recognised in Browne's routes, p. 463, under the names of *Deir* and *Tuggala*, situated in a mountainous region, I have described the ridge above-mentioned, to run to the WNW instead of west. These places, as well as Harraza and Lebeit, (meant for Ibeit,) are placed very much too far to the west of Sennaar, in the map of Mr. Bruce, Vol. V.

journies *westward* from Sennaar; and Mr. Browne informs us, that the people of Bergoo (adjacent to Darfoor) make a practice of going a *slave hunting* into the quarter of Donga. (Travels, p. 473.) Another person amongst those questioned by Mr. Ledyard (implied to come from the same place,) said, that the head of the Nile was situated in his country.* If it be supposed that, in stating the distance of Sennaar from the head of the Nile, they meant that the road lay *through* Darfoor, (which is not improbable) the distance of 55 days would be fully made up. It is reckoned 23 days from Darfoor to Sennaar, and somewhat more from Darfoor to the copper mines of Fertit; which are yet very far short of the head of the White River.

In the map of Africa, 1798, I had placed the head of the White River, about 130 miles to the SE of the place now assigned by Mr. Browne.

Mr. Horneman having again set afloat the idea of the junction of the Niger with the Nile, it becomes necessary to examine, minutely, the geographical materials furnished by Mr. Browne and Mr. Horneman, as well as the notices found in Edrisi; in order to shew the improbability of such a fact. Mr. Horneman was informed by persons who had travelled to Darfoor, that the Niger (*Joliba*) passed by the south of Darfoor, into the White River. It is certain that Herodotus† collected much the same kind of information in Egypt: but it is equally certain that the people whom Mr. Browne consulted at Darfoor, were silent, respecting any such junction: on the contrary, they report, not only that the White River is formed of sources, springing from the mountains on the south, but also that the waters between Darfoor and those mountains, run to the westward. It is

* See Proceed. Afr. Assoc. for 1790, chap. ii.     † Euterpe, c. 32.

proper to add, that the mountains in question, named Kumri, or *Komri*, are, as the name imports, the *Mountains* of the *Moon*; in which Ptolemy, and the Arabian geographers, place the remote head of the Nile.*

In chapter vi. of the Geographical Illustrations, 1798, I have set forth several facts, with a view to shew the probability of the termination of the Niger, by *evaporation*, in the country of Wangara, &c. To that, I shall beg leave to refer: but as many additional facts, tending to strengthen my former ideas, have been furnished by recent travellers, I shall have occasion to repeat some of the former statements and arguments, in the course of the discussion.

Towards the west and SW, to the extent of several hundred miles from the capital of Darfoor, Mr. Browne learnt, that the country was intersected by a number of streams, whose courses pointed to the west and north-west. He appears to speak, however, with less confidence of the courses of all the other waters, save the *Misselâd*, and the small river *Batta*, its adjunct. These, he unequivocally conducts from SE to NW. (See pages 449—464, and his map at page 180). But of the others, he merely says, " the course of the rivers, if rightly given, is, for the most part, from E to W." But he also says, p. 449, " the country they flow through, is said to be, great part of the year, wet and marshy; the heat is excessive, and the people remark that there is no winter." The principal, as well as the most remote of these rivers, is the *Bahr Kulla*, denominated from a country of the same name, described (p. 308), to *abound* with *water*; and this Bahr Kulla is considerable enough to require

* Ptolemy, Afr. Tab. IV. Edrisi, p. 15, *et seq.* Abulfeda, *Prologom.* Article Rivers. *Komri*, or *Kumri*, means *lunar.*

boats to cross it, of which some are made of single trees, large
enough to hold ten persons. *

It would seem, therefore, (if Mr. Browne was correctly informed,
and I can see no reason to doubt, because he speaks with caution),
as if these rivers descended from the high country on the south of
Darfoor, into a comparatively low, and hollow tract to the west, in
which also two large lakes are marked in Mr. Browne's map: and
this tract falls, in our geography, nearly midway between the head
of the White River, and the country of *Wangara*, placed according
to the notices found in Edrisi; and which are corroborated, generally, by Mr. Horneman, who was told that Wangara lay to the
westward of the empire of Bornu. † Through this country of Wangara, the great river of interior Africa (our *Niger*) runs, and beyond
Wangara, eastward, we are unable to *trace* it. (It may be necessary
to remark here, that Edrisi conceived that the Niger ran to the west,
from a source, common to that, and to the Egyptian Nile.)

In fact, one ought not to be surprised to find, considering how very
loosely and inaccurately such kind of information must necessarily
be given, at so great a distance from the seat of inquiry, (that is,
many hundred miles from Mr. Browne's station in Darfoor), if the
lakes and rivers in question should turn out to be those of Wangara.

* I think I perceive in Mr. Browne's description of Darkulla, the traces of an
alluvial country ; that is, one whose soil is formed from the deposition of rivers ;
intersected by their branches ; and periodically inundated. Mr. Browne says of the
natives, " they are very cleanly, to which the *abundance of water* in their country,
contributes. They have ferry-boats on the river, which are impelled by poles, partly
by a double oar, like our canoes. The trees are so large, from the quantity of water
and deep clay, that canoes are hollowed out of them, sufficiently capacious to contain
ten persons." Travels, p. 308, 309.

† So says Leo, p. 254.

itself! It may be observed, that the distances from the capital of Darfoor agree nearly as well to the lakes of Wangara, as to those of *Hermad* and *Dwi;* and the bearing does not differ two points of the compass.* There is nothing to check the bearings from Darfoor, on that side; and it would not be at all extraordinary, if two descriptions, such as those of Edrisi, and of the people of Darfoor, should be even more at variance, than the difference between the positions of the *two sets* of lakes and rivers, on the map.

But how ambiguous soever the subject of the *western* streams, between the head of the White River and Wangara, may be, the waters that flow from the southern and western borders of Darfoor, are clearly known to run to the north-west, and to form a large lake; proving a hollow space to exist, in the quarter, north-west of Darfoor; and little more than 160 miles eastward of Wangara. † Whether this hollow be a continuation of that which receives the waters of the Niger, and forms a part of them into lakes, in Wangara, remains to be discovered. It is, however, in proof, that Edrisi believed the fact, by his describing a water communication the whole way. I now proceed to describe the course of these waters, that flow from the quarter of Darfoor, towards the north-west.

Mr. Browne was informed, (page 449,) that on the south of Darfoor, and between that country and the source of the White River, the waters formed a considerable river, named *Misselád.* This he traces on his map at page 180, and in the routes given in his Appendix, p. 449, 464, 468, towards the NNW and NW, to a point above the parallel of 15 degrees north (*i. e.* through near 400 G.

---

* See the General Map of North Africa, at page 178.

† For Edrisi, page 13, places this lake (Kauga,) at ten journies eastward of Semegonda in Wangara.

miles of course); but he is silent, otherwise than by implication, respecting its future course. But of a second river (the *Batta*) whose course lies *between* the Misselâd and Darfoor, and very near to the former, he says, that it flows from the *south*, and then, deviating to the *west*, it falls into the *Bahr-el-Fittré*. (P. 464). It remains to be added, that, following the western road from Wara to Bagherme (in his Appendix, p. 464, 465), we come to the Bahr Fittré itself: but without any notices respecting the crossing of the Misselâd river, by the way. This matter, however, will be made clearer, presently, by the aid of Horneman and Edrisi.

Mr. Browne continues to say, (p. 465,) that "the people on the banks of the Bahr Fittré use little boats, for the purpose of passing from one place to another, on *the river*." The word *Bahr* indicating equally a lake or a river, is here understood for the *latter*, by Mr. Browne; but we learn from Mr. Horneman, that the dominions of the sultan of *Fiddri*, (as he writes it,) are situated round a large freshwater lake, which bears the same name: and that, into this lake flows *a river which comes from Darfoor ;* and whose banks are very rich in sugar-canes. (See above, p. 115.)

This account of the lake is strengthened by several circumstances. Horneman says, that the district of Fiddri, although so named by its own inhabitants, is called *Cougu,* or *Cugu,* by the people who dwell eastward; (the Arabs;) *Luffe,* by those on the west. Now, *Couga,* or *Kauga,* is noted by Edrisi, as a country and city near a large lake of fresh water, situated at 30 journies westward, or southwestward, from Dongola; 36 eastward from Gana: and here we have the very position. Moreover, Mr. Browne describes, in the before-mentioned western route, at $3\frac{1}{2}$ journies short of the Bahr

Fittré, *Dar Cooka,*\* doubtless the country of *Couga* or *Cugu* in question.

The circumstance of boats plying on the Bahr Fittré (Browne's Travels, p. 465,) also accords with the idea of a lake. Nor can there be a doubt that the Misselâd of Browne, is the river from the quarter of Darfoor, intended by Horneman: and that *it*, as well as the river of Batta, falls into the lake of Fittré. †

It may be remarked, that what Edrisi describes as the upper part of the course of the *Niger*, (*Nilus Nigrorum*) is evidently intended for this river: but he describes it as originating from the same source as the *Egyptian Nile*, and flowing westward. There also appears in Ptolemy, the same river springing from about the 10th degree of north latitude; as the Misselâd does.

It appears certain then, that the ground declines, from the quarter of Darfoor, towards the interior of Africa, to the north-west and west: and the descriptions of Edrisi, (page 13,) go equally to prove that the ground also declines from the NE to SW, towards the lake of Fittré; because he describes the river of *Kuku* to run southward. ‡

\* Here we have a proof that the Eastern people call *Fittré* by the name of *Kauga,* (or *Cooka,*) as Horneman says. *Dar* has been explained by Mr. Browne to mean *country;* as *Dar-Fûr*, the country of Fûr, or Foor.

† This lake is said by Mr. Horneman, page 118, to be from four to eight journies in circuit; varying its dimensions with the dry or the rainy season; thus increasing threefold with the rains, and leaving, in the dry season, an enriched soil to the husbandman.

‡ This seems to be the river mentioned by Ibn al Wardi, (in Hartman's Edrisi, p. 62,) as coming from the east, and passing by Ghama (read Begama, or Begarmé,) into the *Nile;* meaning the Nile of the Negroes, (our Niger.)

The same must be understood of the river of the Antelopes, or *Wad-el-Gazel*, which is marked by Mr. Browne, (p. 465,) at two journies to the NW of the lake Fittré; and by Mr. Beaufoy at the distance of one journey from the capital of Bournu. Mr. Horneman indeed was told, that the Wad-el-Gazel was not a river, but a fruitful and well inhabited valley. It is probably both : that is, a fertile valley, with a river running through it. Hence we must suppose the Wad-el-Gazel to be another river that falls into the lake Fittré, from the north ; and consequently, the lake itself, to be the receptacle of the eastern waters of the interior of North Africa.

Edrisi places Semegonda at ten journies to the westward or SW of *Kauga*, (our *Fittré*,) and within the country of Wangara, which is entirely surrounded by the branches of the Niger, and periodically inundated by its waters : and it is clear that he believed, that there was a water communication between Wangara and Kauga; because he says, (p. 7.) that salt was conveyed all along the Niger, eastward to that point. It may be remarked, that Horneman says, that the people of Fittré (Kauga) have no salt, but what they obtain from vegetable substances.*

* It should be observed, that Edrisi, (p. 13,) reckons Kauga to the country of Wangara ; although some, says he, reckon it to belong to *Kanem.*

It is proper in this place to restate and correct the line of distance between *Gana* and *Dongola;* which will be found in the Proceed. Afr. Assoc. for 1798, p. 122. There it appears, that Kauga is given by Edrisi, at 30 journies, equal on his scale, to 570 G. miles from Dongola ; and it is found by Mr. Browne's statement, to fall at 578. Again, Mr. Horneman says, that Fittré, (or Kauga,) is 40 journies to the eastward of Kashna, (See above, p. 138.) This interval of distance, taking Kashna as it is placed in the Map of 1798, is 653 G. miles ; equal to 16⅓ per day ; and is perfectly satisfactory. Edrisi allows 36 journies between Gana and Kauga ; so that by this account, Gana ought to be nearer to Kauga, by four journies, than Kashna is. In the Map of 1798, Gana is placed eight miles too far to the east. (See the

If there be, as Edrisi says, (page 7,) a water communication between Kauga and Wangara, (no matter which way the water runs),
the fact of a common level, would, of course, be proved; and then
it must be admitted to be highly improbable, that any part of the
course of the White River, southward of Darfoor, should be on a
lower level, than the lake of Fittré. But, perhaps, some may doubt
the authority of Edrisi, in this point; and possibly, the more so,
since he says, that the Niger runs to the west.

But placing this circumstance out of the question, and leaving
the facts set forth by Mr. Browne and Mr. Horneman, to speak for
themselves, it may be asked,

Proceed. p. 121.) This corrected, Gana will be 82 from Kashna; which, however,
is still too much for four journies, and agrees better to five.

The interval thus corrected, between Gana and Kauga, is 575 G. miles in *direct
distance;* which allows no more than 15½ per day, for Edrisi's 36 days; whilst his
ordinary scale is 19. If therefore, the report of Edrisi is right, Gana must either lie
more to the west, or the course of the Niger, along which his route leads, to within
ten journies of Kauga, must form a very deep curve to the south, after passing the
dominions of Houssa, (of which Gana makes a part.) That it does decline to the
south, Mr. Horneman was repeatedly informed, as may be seen above, pages 115,
117, but whether in a degree sufficient to occasion the difference above-mentioned,
is not ascertained.

M. D'Anville also had an idea, and so describes it in his Map of Africa, 1749,
(possibly from actual information), that the Niger declined to the south beyond
Gana; so that the termination of it, in the lake of Semegonda, was 3¼ degrees of
latitude to the south of Gana; and which, by the bye, would place the lake of Semegonda, about the same parallel with the *Bahr Hemad* of Mr. Browne. At present,
however, we must be content with proportioning the distance between Gana and
Kauga; which, admitting a curvature to the south, allows a rate of 16⅓ or 16½; or
that of ordinary caravan travelling. It has been shewn that Horneman's report of
the distance between Kashna and Fittré, is very consistent: and there can be no
question, that, of the two, we ought to prefer Horneman's report, from its being less
subject to error than the other, which has passed through so many hands, in its
way to us.

1. Whether it is probable that the Niger, after running about 2250 British miles in direct distance from its source, should not have arrived at a lower level, than that of the countries adjacent to the heads of the Nile?*

2. Whether the course of the Misselâd river, from the south of Darfoor, is not almost directly contrary to that which the Niger should take from Wangara, in order to join the White River?

3. Whether the course of the waters, to the west of Darfoor, and of the head of the White River, are not also reported to run *towards* the quarter that contains the Niger, instead of *coming from it?* and are they not said to run through a wet marshy country; whilst that to the east, in the line between Fittré and the White River, is high and mountainous?†

4. Has not the country of Wangara, &c. like that of Fittré, the character of an alluvial tract, inundated by the periodical floods of the Niger, to the extent of more than 350 British miles in length, by more than 170 in breadth: and has not both that and Gana,

* The Thames, between Maidenhead Bridge and Mortlake, (about 41 B. miles in a straight line,) has a fall of rather more than one foot eight inches in each mile. But this is a *smooth* part of its course : for although the Thames does not, by any means, spring from very elevated lands, it cannot be supposed to fall less than four feet in each mile, taken on its whole course. On this idea, the Niger should have a fall of more than 8000 feet, in its supposed course to the White River. But even if two feet and a half (which appears very moderate indeed) be allowed, the fall would be no less than 5625 feet, or 115 yards more than an English mile. Is it to be credited, that the bed of the White River, on the south of Darfoor, and at a point not very remote from its source, is a mile lower than the springs of the Joliba, or Niger?

† Browne's Travels, page 473.

large fresh water lakes in the dry season?* May not so great an extent of surface, suffice for the evaporation of the waters of the Niger; as we have already an instance of the kind in Persia, in which the *Heermend*, a river of more than 400 miles length of course, is evaporated in less than $\frac{1}{20}$ part of the surface of the inundation formed in Wangara?† I now return to the general geography.

Mr. Horneman, in describing the position of the southern states, speaks of *Wadey*, bordering on the west of Darfoor; then *Metho*, west, (or rather NW) of Wadey; both of which are watered by the river which flows from Darfoor to the lake Fittré, *(i. e.* the *Misselâd)*; and, finally, Fittré itself, to the NW of Metho. Continuing the description—*Begarmé* ‡ is said to lie N of Wadey; Bournu, N of Fittré. *Bergoo* seems not to have been known to Horneman; or, perhaps, he may have confounded it with the Burgu

---

* Edrisi says, " Ab urbe Ghana ad primos limites terræ Vancáræ est iter octo dierum (orientem versus)—Atque hæc eadem est insula longitudinis trecentorum milliarium, centum et quinquaginta latitudinis, quam Nilus undequaque circundat toto anni tempore. Adveniente verò mense Augusto, et æstu gravescente, Niloque inundante, insula ista vel certè major pars illius aquis obruitur, manetque sepulta aquis quamdiu Nilus terram inundare consuevit." (Sionita, p. 11 and 12. See also Hartmann's Edrisi, article Vankara, p. 47 *et seq.*

† Ebn Haukal, an Arabian geographer, of the tenth century, (lately translated by Sir William Ouseley,) gives the following account of the river *Heermend*, p. 205.

" The most considerable river of *Sejestan* is the *Heermend*, which comes from Ghaur to the city of *Bost*, and from that runs to *Sejestan*, to the lake *Zareh*. This lake is very small when the waters of the river are not copious ; when the river is full, the lake increases accordingly. The length of this lake is about 30 farsangs, (about 110 B. miles,) and in breadth about one *merhilch*. (Day's journey, or 24 B. miles.) Its waters are sweet, wholesome, &c."

It is well known, that there is no *outlet* from the lake Zareh.

‡ Begama of Edrisi.

towards Augila (the *Berdoa* of Delisle and D'Anville). Bergoo, according to Mr. Browne, is an independent country: Metho and Wadey, the same: so that the empire of Bournu ends with Fittré (or *Cooka*) Margi, and Wangara, southward.*

Of these countries, Mr. Browne had not heard of Wangara, under that name;† nor of Wadey, or Metho; although he describes the tract which contains them, in his map. Nor does *Dar Cooka* appear to have been known to him, as the Kauga of Edrisi, or as the Fittré of Horneman.

At the capital of Bournu, the interesting inquiries of Mr. Browne end, northward: but as those of Mr. Horneman extend to the borders of Darfoor, they of course *overlap* each other; so as to give much greater authority to the report of the course of the waters from Darfoor to the lake Fittré.

With respect to the line of distance, between Fezzan and Darfoor; Darfoor and Sennaar; these are the details: (that from Gana to Dongola, has been already given, page 188.)

Mr. Beaufoy allows between Temissa (in Fezzan) and the capital of *Bournu*, 43 days of caravan travelling, in a south-easterly direction. Mr. Browne places the same capital, deduced from inquiries made at Darfoor, in lat. 19° 45′, lon. 21° 33′; so as to leave an interval

---

* Mr. Browne, (page 473,) states the distance between *Donga*, and the (*southern*) limit of Bornu, to be 20 journies.

† Mr. Horneman's informant called it *Ungara;* and it appears that the Arabs name it *Belad-el-Tebr*, or the country of gold. (Herbelot and Bakui.) Mr. Browne was told, in Darfoor, that gold was not found in any quantity, to the west. But Wangara, a country of gold, at least in former times, lies to the west of Darfoor !

of distance equal to 562 G. miles, between Temissa and Bournu; giving a rate of only 13 miles and a small fraction, *per* day. This rate falls far short of caravan travelling; and it is possible that the halting days may have been included in the aggregate number 43; as is often done, when the inquiries are not sufficiently pointed. In the Proceed. Afr. Assoc. 1798, it is stated, that Bornou falls at 534 G. miles from Dongola on the Nile; and Mr. Browne's result gives about 600. It should, however, be noted, that Mr. Browne's Tables (page 467), give a bearing of N ¼ W between Begarmé and Bournu, which I have followed in preference to his map, where it is N 13 W; and thus place Bournu at 562 from Dongola. A mean between the position in the former map, and that given by Mr. Browne, would be 567. But through the want of a cross line of distance, that can be depended on, the position of this important point in geography, remains in uncertainty. Mr. Horneman was told that Bournu was 15 days journey from Kashna: and at 25, in a W by S direction, short of Fittré. This is, no doubt, meant of the *boundary* of the empire of Bournu, towards Kashna, and not of the capital; and this report appears very probable, as the Bournuan dominions are said to terminate on that side, with the country of Wangara.

# CHAPTER IV.

*Concerning the Tribes that occupy the habitable Parts of the Great Desert.—Tibbo and Tuarick.—Empires of Bournu, Asben, and Houssa.—General Observations.*

THE inquiries of Mr. Horneman throw some new light on the distribution of the habitable tracts, inclosed by, or adjoining to, that part of the Sahara which lies to the east of Tombuctoo; as well as of the tract that stands in the same relation to the Eastern, or *Libyan* Desert.

The empires of Houssa and Bournou, consisting of various lesser states, appear to divide the space along the Niger, from the quarter of Tombuctoo, to that of Darfoor, eastward; and to extend a considerable way to the north, beyond the general line of the river.

Two considerable nations, also, the TIBBO and TUARICK, appear to divide the remainder of the space, northward, *within* the Deserts; embracing Fezzan on every side but the north; and closing on the maritime states along the Mediterranean, from the Desert which shuts up Egypt on the west, to Mount Atlas. Mr. Horneman appears to be the first person who has given these general ideas of the Tibbo and Tuarick; and they merit attention.

The Tibbo, or Tibboo, possess the eastern, and the Tuarick the western, and most extensive part of this vast tract. Fezzan separates them on the north: and its meridian forms nearly their common boundary, until they close southward on Kashna and Bournu.*

According to Mr. Horneman, the settlements of the Tibbo, begin at the south and south-east of Fezzan, and extend from thence eastward, along the south of the Harutsch and of the Augilan Desert, to the wide sandy Desert of the Lebetæ† (*Libya*), which shuts up Egypt, on the west. This Desert forms the eastern boundary of the Tibbo. On the south, wandering Arabs possess the tract between them and the empire of Bournu; and on the west, are the Tuarick of Asben (Agades), Tagazee, &c.

The Tibbo are said to be divided into the following tribes: 1. Rshade, or *Rock* Tibbo. 2. Febabo. 3. Burgu, or Birgu. 4. Arna. 5. Bilma. 6. Nomadic Tibbo.

1. *The Rshade.* This tribe possesses the country adjoining to the south and south-east of Fezzan; and is besides intermixed with the Fezzaners, in those quarters of Fezzan, (as the Tuarick are in

* There is a town named *Taboo*, a considerable way to the SW of Fezzan. D'Anville writes it *Tibedou*. It seems to be the *Tabidium* of Pliny, one of the towns conquered by the Romans, under Balbus. (Pliny, lib. v. c. 4 and 5.) Pliny says, c. 8. that " the Romans possessed the country, even to the river Niger, which separates *Africa* from *Ethiopia*;" and gives a long list of provinces and towns subject to them. It may be conceived, that besides Fezzan, Gadamis, Taboo, &c. they possessed the fertile tract, in the line from thence to the Niger; that is, Agadez, Kashna, and perhaps Gana.

It may be remarked that Pliny (c. 8) speaks of TWO *Ethiopias;* and quotes Homer, as having divided them into *Eastern* and *Western*. One may conceive that the division between them, was the fertile tract in question, extending from Fezzan, in the line towards the Niger. † *Levata* of Leo, page 245.

the western quarters, and the Arabs in the north.)  The towns of
the Rock Tibbo, are Abo and Tibesty; which I am enabled to place
generally, by means of a route given by Mr. Horneman.*

The Tibbo *Rshade*, or *Rock* Tibbo, are so denominated from
their building their habitations under rocks, or living in *caves*; before which they build huts of rushes, for their summer's residence.

Some idea of the tract inhabited by this tribe, may be collected
from Mr. Beaufoy's account of the country between Fezzan and
Bournu, ch. vi.; and from Mr. Horneman's description of the white
Harutsch.  The road to Bournu leads out of the country of Fezzan,
from Temissa; from which town, seven journies bring us to the
plain of *Tibesty*, said to be inhabited by Mahomedans; which is
indeed the religion of the Rock Tibbo.  The last four days lead
across what is termed " a hilly desert of sand."  So far Mr.
Beaufoy's informant.

The white Harutsch, crossed by Mr. Horneman, is in this vicinity, and extends southward, from the line of his route across it,
from Augila to Mourzouk: so that it is not improbable that the

* From Mourzouk to Gatron, (or Kattron,) south 54 miles; understood to be
of British standard, and to include the windings of the road.  Thence to Tegerhie,
SSW 33 miles.  To Abo 7 days; and thence to Tibesty, 3 days in an easterly direction.  Finally, to Burgu, 18 days; each of which 28 days are reckoned 18 B. miles
*by the road.* See above, page 107.

It has been calculated in page 155, that Teghery, by the general result of the
authorities, should be placed S 26 W, 68 G. miles from Mourzouk.

From thence, the 10 days to Tibesty, in an easterly direction, may be taken at
about 140 G. miles; which meeting the line of 7 days, equal to 98 G. miles from
Temissa, (See Proceed. Afr. Assoc. 1790, chap. iv.) places Tibesty at 133 miles SE
by E. from Mourzouk.

" hilly desert" just mentioned, is a continuation of the white Harutsch. What renders it more probable is, that Mr. Horneman was
told, that certain *black* mountains, which he suspected to be a part
of the black Harutsch, are crossed in the way from Fezzan to
Bournu. And it has been shewn, that the black Harutsch adjoins
to the white Harutsch on the east ; and this arrangement may continue, southward : in which direction Mr. Horneman was informed
the black Harutsch stretched, beyond the line of his route.

This gentleman describes the hilly part of the white Harutsch to
consist of " *loose friable limestone,* in which the petrifactions are *imbedded so loosely,* that they may be taken out with ease." No rocks
therefore are more likely to contain natural caves, or are more easily
excavated, when wanted. This tract, therefore, seems, as well from
description, as position, to be that inhabited by the Rock Tibbo.

A circumstance in Herodotus ( Melpom. 183), leads one to conclude, that these are the *Ethiopian Troglodytæ, hunted by the Garamantes.* The Garamantes, I trust, I have made to appear, are the
Fezzaners ; and here are a tribe of Troglodytæ, on their very borders. They are said, in the same place, to be very swift of foot.
Mr. Horneman says, that the walk of the Tibbos is light and swift ;
as if remarkably so : but then he speaks of the Tibbo, collectively ;
and not of any particular tribe. But, on the other hand, it appears
that he saw more of the Rock Tibbo, than any other : for he says,
" they go in multitudes to Fezzan ;" and it may be that his opinion
of the nation at large was, in a great measure, formed by what he
saw of this tribe. *

* The *Troglodytæ* were found in every place where nature or art had prepared
recesses for them ; and are always gifted with superior swiftness of foot. In particular, in Pliny, lib. vii. c. 2. and in Hanno's Voyage, &c.

Considering that *Fezzan,* under the name of *Garamanta,* was one of the earliest

A strange particular is related of the Troglodytæ, by Herodotus. He says, that their language bears some resemblance to the scream- ing of bats.* Melpom. 183.

2. *The Febabo.* This tribe is found at 10 journies SSW from Augila; between which territories, on the side of Augila, is a desert of 6 journies, void of water. And notwithstanding this circumstance, and the distance from the sea coast of Bengasi (20 days, at least), they are annually exposed to the depredations of the people of Ben- gasi, who, joined with those of Augila, go to *steal* men and dates. See above, on Gegabib, page 148.

3. *Burgu, or Birgu.* (This must not be mistaken for Bergoo, a state situated in the quarter of Darfoor.) It appears in D'Anville and Delisle, as well as in Leo, under the name of *Berdoa;* but the name is too often repeated by Mr. Horneman to be a mistake of his. This tribe resides to the south of Febabo, at the distance of *some* days; and at eighteen, eastward from Tibesty. Hence the Burgu tribe may be placed S a little W from Augila, and about the parallel of the south of Fezzan.

Their territory is said to be fertile, but they bear the character of

known inland countries of Africa, to the Greeks, it is not altogether improbable that the first idea of the characteristic swiftness of the *Ethiopian Troglodytæ,* was derived from thence. And considering also the false idea entertained by the Greeks, of the bearing of the western side of Africa, Hanno might have supposed the source of the river *Lixus,* the reported seat of *his* Troglodytæ, to have been situated in the centre of Africa.

* Horneman was told by the Augilans, that the Tibbo of Febabo, or Burgu, (it is not clear which) spoke a language that resembled the *whistling* of birds. He also takes occasion to remark, what Herodotus says concerning the language of the Ethi- opians, hunted by the *Garamantes* ; but probably without referring these last to the country of Fezzan.

robbers. A caravan of Fezzanners, from Begarmé and Bournu, about the time of Mr. Horneman's visit, was plundered by them. The Sultan of Fezzan sent a force to punish them ; the smallness of which, seems to prove that the Burgu are either not numerous, or are very much dispersed. (See above, page 107). The route of the Sultan's army helps to fix the positions both of Burgu, and of the Rock Tibbo.*

Mr. Beaufoy relates (ch. iv. 1790,) that on another occasion, the Tibbo of Tibesty plundered a caravan of Fezzan, which robbery was also punished : but on the last occasion, the Tibestians (who are the Rock Tibbo), aided the Sultan. It appears by the geography, that the caravans from the SE are much exposed to the Burgu and Tibesty, in their route to Fezzan.†

* It appears in page 176, (*note*) that Burgu is 18 journies from Tibesty ; which, at 14 G. miles each, (as they are of 18 B. miles by the road,) produce 252 miles. Burgu is said, page 119, to be situated to the south, *some days* distant from Febabo. On the construction the line of 252 miles passes to the eastward of Febabo, (placed at 10 days to SSW from Augila, see page 108,) *so far*, as to place Burgu to the *south-eastward*, instead of *south*, from Febabo. It may be, that Febabo does not bear so far to the west, as SSW from Augila ; as less than 14 miles per day cannot well be allowed, from Tibesty. I have therefore altered the bearing from SSW, and made it somewhat nearer to the meridian. The Berdoa, or Bardeo of Leo, (pages 245, 246,) agrees to this position, 500 Arabic miles from the Nile, in the midst of the Desert of Libya ; and abounding with dates.

† Notwithstanding the appearance of retributive justice in these attacks on the Tibbo, by the Sultan of Fezzan, yet Mr. Horneman lets us a little into the secret, by informing us, (page 68,) that " for some years past, the Sultan has augmented his revenues considerably, by *cursory expeditions* against the Tibbos of Burgu." And the result of the above expedition was, " the *stealing* of about two hundred people, which were sold," &c. It may be remarked, that Mr. Browne says of the Sultan of Dar-foor, that a part of his revenue arises from a participation in the profits of the *selatia*, or *slave-hunting* parties. (page 299.) And of the Negro country of *Dar Kulla*, he says,

4. *Arna.* This tribe is said to live five or six journies to the eastward of the Burgu; and must therefore border on the sandy Desert of the *Lebetæ.* Mr. Horneman appears to have known them only by name.

5. *Bilma.* This is the principal tribe of the Tibbo. They occupy the middle space, between Fezzan and Bournu, adjacent to the great Desert of Bilma. Their capital of *Dyrke* is said to be one journey from Bilma; which may be the Balmala of Edrisi. They carry on a commerce between Bournu and Fezzan. (See above, p. 106.) The *Billa* of Ptolemy may possibly be meant for Bilma; but is too far to the eastward.

Mr. Beaufoy states the distance to be 45 days of the salt caravans from Agadez to the lake of Dumboo; which is situated within the Desert of Bilma. These, at 13 G. miles per day,\* give a total of 585 miles. The interval on the construction is about 60 less. Either then, Agadez is more to the west, or Dumboo more to the east. Two circumstances render it probable that Agadez should be more to the west: Mr. Magrah was told that it lay S 30° W from Fezzan: and that it lay N from Kashna. That part of the General Map of 1798, has not been altered.

that even the public regulations are framed with a view to the *entrapping* of individuals for slaves. (308.) So that the slave trade exists much in the same manner, in this quarter of Africa, where none of the slaves are purchased by European traders, as in the west.

\* It has appeared that the caravan travellers in stating the time between distant places, are apt to give the whole time that elapses between their leaving one place, and arriving at another. Hence the days of halt, have often been added to the days of march ; and a faulty route of travelling has thence been adopted. This, no doubt, occasioned the low rate adopted, soon after the institution of the Association : and which nothing but actual experiment can effectually correct.

6. *Nomadic Tibbo.* These are the most southerly of the tribes; and are seated in the *Bahr-el-Gazel*, which, Mr. Horneman was told, was a long and fruitful valley, 7 journies north of Begarmé. Of the *Bahr* (or *Wad*)-el-Gazel, I have already spoken, in page 168. The distance of 7 journies N of Begarmé would place the Nomadic Tibbo within the empire of Bournu. Perhaps, in Bournu, as in Persia, both ancient and modern, Nomadic tribes find plenty of room:* but whether so far southward, may be a doubt, for a river of the name of Wad-el-Gazel, is said to flow even into the Desert of Bilma. Antelopes are found in the neighbourhood of Dumboo; and there may be a river denominated from them, in that quarter, as well as in that of Begarmé.

## *Of the* TUARICK.†

These, whom Mr. Horneman styles a *mighty* people, appear to occupy the habitable parts of the Great Sahara, situated to the west of the meridian of Fezzan. They must necessarily be widely dispersed; and they are also divided into many tribes. Mr. Horneman very properly confines himself to what he *knew*, concerning them: and this knowledge related to little more than to the tribes of *Kolluvi* and *Hagara*, who live the nearest to Fezzan; and carry on a commerce between that place, Soudan, and Gadamis.

The Kolluvi possess (from recent conquest, it would seem,) the

---

* The proof of this fact is most satisfactorily established, by Herodotus, and by Ibn Haukel, a geographical writer of the tenth century, whose work has been lately translated by Sir William Ouseley; to whose labours the science of Geography is much indebted.

† Mr. Horneman regards this nation as the *Terga* of Leo, situated in the western quarter of the Great Desert. (Leo, page 245.)

country of Agadez; which, with other provinces adjacent, forms a state named collectively, *Asben.* It adjoins to Kashna (a part of the empire of Houssa,) on the south; Bournu on the east. Its capital is the city of Agadez, said, by Mr. Magrah's informant, to be in size equal to the suburbs of Tunis; which, Mr. Magrah observes, compose the largest proportion of that city.

But it would appear by the *Soudan* route, transmitted by that gentleman, that the establishments of the Tuarick in other places, as Gazer, Tagazee, Jenet, &c. consisted only of small villages, scattered through an immensity of space: indeed, like most of the other tribes situated within this singular region Zanfara and Guber, which are said to lie adjacent, pay a tribute to Asben.

The Hagara are the most easterly of the Tuarick, and are near Fezzan. These I am not able to place on the Map: possibly, they either occupy Ganat, on the south of Fezzan; or, as the Tuarick possess Jenet and Sockna, on the NW of it, the town of Agaree, in the same quarter, may be the Hagara meant. It appears in the routes collected by Mr. Magrah, at Tunis.

Mr. Horneman also mentions, but without any notice of situation, the *Matkara* tribe: also that of *Tagama,* situated towards Tombuctoo and Soudan.* He forms an ingenious conjecture respecting this tribe. They are said to be whiter than the rest of the Africans of the interior (or rather, perhaps, less black); and are *not* Mahometans. Now, as the term *Nazary,* or Christian, is applied generally to those whom the Mahometans call unbelievers, Mr. Horneman

* Ptolemy has a city named *Tagama,* at the Niger, but too far to the east, to answer to the position here given. (Afr. Tab. IV.). There is also a *Tegoma* in our geography, near Kashna.

infers that this circumstance has given rise to the report of there being a tribe of *white Christians* near Tombuctoo.*

The eastern Tuarick live chiefly a Nomadic life.

One curious particular relating to the Tuarick is, that they have formed colonies in *Siwah*, *Augila*, and *Sockna*; all of which are commercial places, forming a chain along the northern border of the Libyan Desert, towards the maritime states along the Mediterranean. To these, the *Lesser* Oasis is to be added, in course; as speaking the same language as Siwah; and this is corroborated by Mr. Browne, who says (page 132), that the Lesser Oasis forms a kind of capital settlement of the Muggrebine Arabs. Gadamis also may possibly be found to be a colony of the same people; whose establishments of this kind, may extend along the northern border of the whole Sahara; since they have colonies in a quarter so remote from their own nation.†

The Tuarick are said, by Mr. Horneman, to be a very interesting people; the most so, of any of the tribes of the Sahara: but he gives the palm of intelligence, benevolence, and mildness, to the people of Houssa; who are, however, Negroes.

* Many persons have expected to find in the interior of Africa, the remains of the Carthaginian nation, expelled by the Romans. Considering, however, the vast interval of time that has elapsed, we can hardly expect to find the remnant of a nation, continuing so far unmixed with the surrounding nations, as to preserve their distinction of character and language. Besides, it would really seem as if the Carthaginians themselves, (meaning the descendants of the Phœnicians,) were not to be regarded as as a *nation*, so much as *bodies* of *citizens*, inhabiting commercial towns: so that their language may never have prevailed generally over Barbary.

† Mr. Browne (page 232) denominates the people of the *Greater* Oasis, *Muggrebine* Arabs, as well as those of the *Lesser*. It is probable then, that all the Oases are colonies of the *Tuarick*.

This Houssa, (or *Haussa*, as Mr. Horneman calls it), whose position has so long evaded geographical research, is, according to this gentleman, an *empire*, consisting of a number of lesser states, in the very centre of North Africa. Kashna, or Kasna, which has so long figured on the Map as an independent empire, must, according to his description, (and which is very consistent), give way to Houssa, of which Kasna is no more than a province. He includes in Houssa, on the authority of a Maraboot, the countries situated generally between Tombuctoo, Asben, and Bournu.*

He says that three names are applied to this empire (as to Fittré :) Haussa, the name among the people themselves; Soudan,† (meaning the country of the *Blacks*, or Negroes) by the Arabs; and Asna, by the people of Bournu. But this last, he says, in strictness, applies only to the countries of Kasna, Kano, (Gana,) and such parts of

---

* See the sketch opposite to page 111.

† The Moors and Arabs call the country of the Negroes, which was designed by the Romans under the name of *Nigritia*, SOUDAN. Abulfeda includes all the known part of Africa, south of the Great Desert, in BELAD SOUDAN, or the country of Soudan. (The word *Souda* or *Suda*, in Arabic, signifies *black*.)

Mr. Browne, who had visited a part of Soudan, namely *Darfoor*, agrees that Soudan corresponds to our *Nigritia;* being " a general term for the country of the Blacks." (page 182.) In his preface, page xxv. he says that " nothing can be more vague, than the use of the word Soudan, or Sudan. Among the Egyptians and Arabs, *Ber-es-Soudan* is the place where the caravans arrive, when they reach the first habitable part of *Dar-Fûr:* but that country seems its *eastern extremity;* for I never heard it applied to Kordofân or Sennaar. It is used equally in Dar-Fûr to express the country to the west ; but on the whole, seems ordinarily applied to signify that part of the land of the Blacks nearest Egypt."

It has been seen, however, that the people of Tunis and Fezzan, reckon Houssa, that is, Kashna, and the adjacent countries, to Soudan ; whence it must be extended westward to Tombuctoo, at least. Whether it ought to be extended farther west, I know not. The term, which is of Arabic origin, may possibly have in its application, a limited range, and may not embrace the entire country of the Negroes.

Houssa, as lie to the eastward of *these* : in effect, those parts of Houssa which border on, or are nearest to, the Bournuans : a practice that has prevailed, more or less, in every country.

Concerning the existence of *a city* of Houssa, Mr. Horneman is silent : but he learnt that Tombuctoo (between which, however, and Fezzan, there is very little intercourse,) is certainly the principal city, and most worthy of notice, in the interior of Africa.

It must be admitted that the information collected by Mr. Magrah, at Tunis, respecting Houssa, agrees with the report of Mr. Horneman ; but still there may also be a *city* of the name of Houssa, in the quarter towards Tombuctoo, and within the limits of the empire now denominated Houssa ; and which city, at an earlier period, may have been the capital of the empire.

Mr. Magrah says, (Beaufoy's MSS.) " All my late informants persist in representing Houssa as a considerable empire, comprehending many principalities. Kasna, (says Sidi Cossem,) is the *great city*, Houssa, the *country* of the Negroes. The course from Tunis to Gadamis is due south ; and the same from thence to Houssa." (The same authority gave the bearing from Fezzan to Agades, at S 30° W. ; and thence to Kasna, due south.)*

* The following information occurs in a letter from Mr. Jackson of Santa Cruz, to Mr. Willis, dated 1st of July, 1797.

" I have informed myself particularly concerning Houssa, and I find there is no such place. The environs of all great towns are called in the Arabic of this country, *El Huz*, or *Huza.*'

## GENERAL OBSERVATIONS.

IT is an unquestionable fact, that Geography has gained very considerably by Mr. Horneman's travels; though not quite so much as if he had transmitted the general bearings of the different portions of his routes; as well as the latitudes of some important geographical points; together with an account of the time employed between Fezzan and Tripoly. However, very great allowances must be made, for the critical situation in which he was placed; from the difficulty of supporting the character he had assumed, whilst he was forwarding the purposes of the Association.

It may be justly remarked, that the course of a few years, has solved many of the questions respecting the geography and natural history of Africa, that appeared the most important and curious, during a series of ages : and it may be added, that the physical geography of Africa, turns out to be more remarkable than was even supposed.

Of the questions either wholly, or in part, solved, may be reckoned the following :

*First.* The general direction of the stream of the *Niger*, now proved by Mr. Park, to be from west to east; although the *place* and *mode* of its termination, are not *exactly known*.

*Secondly.* The place of the remote head of the Nile ; in all ages a *desideratum* : and which, although it has not been actually visited, may fairly be believed, on the authority of Mr. Browne's information : more especially, as it agrees so nearly with the report of the Darfoor people, to Ledyard, at Cairo; with the reports of the Arabian geographers ; and with the information collected by M. Maillet, in Egypt.

*Thirdly*. The place of the Oasis, and remains of the temple of Jupiter Ammon ; discovered by Mr. Browne, and corroborated by Mr. Horneman: as also, the exact position and extent of the Greater Oasis, by Mr. Browne; and the approximated position of the Lesser Oasis, by the joint inquiries of the same gentlemen.

*Fourthly*. The position of the nation called *Garamantes* by the ancients ; derived from information collected by the African Association.

*Fifthly*. The truth of the question respecting the *Lotus ;* which, considered fairly, and stripped of the poetical ideas annexed to it, is really what the ancients described it to be. The merit of this discovery, or at least, the distinct proof of it, rests, in a great measure, with Mr. Park.

*Sixthly*. The proof of certain facts stated by the ancients ; as,

1. The Dates of the distant inland tracts, being gathered by the people of the sea coast.

2. The *Mons Ater* of Pliny, recognised in the *Black Harutsch.*

3. The site of Memphis, before involved in doubt and obscurity.

4. The singular conformation of the Mound of *Bubastis*, in Lower Egypt, proved by the French *Sçavans*.*

Although a part, only, of these discoveries, have been made by persons employed by the Association, yet it is probable that the gentleman to whom we owe some of the most brilliant of them, was in part determined to the pursuit, by the discussions set on foot by the Association ; which had been established some years before Mr. Browne's travels commenced.

* The reader is requested to compare the description of this Mound in Herodotus, (Euterpe, 137, 138,) with that in the Voyage on the Tanitic branch of the Nile, in the *Mémoires sur L'Egypte*, p, 215, *et seq*. See also the Geog. System of Herodotus, p. 513, for the application.

# POSTSCRIPT.

WHEN the above Memoir was printed, I was ignorant that the following passage occurred, in Mr. Horneman's Letter of the 6th April, from Mourzouk.

" I spoke to a man who had seen Mr. Browne in Darfoor: he gave me some information respecting the countries he travelled through, and told me, that the communication of the Niger with the Nile, was not to be doubted, but that this communication before the rainy season, was very little; in those parts, the Niger being at the dry period *reposing*, or *non fluens*."

If the authority is to be depended on, it proves two facts: first, that the *Niger* and *Nile*, (that is the *western* branch, or *White* River), are by no means one and the same river; but, on the contrary, that their fountains are perfectly distinct: for, it is agreed on all hands, that the White River is a very large stream, at all seasons; whereas, we are here told that the Niger discharges into the Nile, during the dry season, only a very small portion of its waters: consequently, the waters of the Nile must come from some other quarter than the Niger.

The other fact is, that during the dry season, the waters of the Niger are generally evaporated in the inland country: a fact disbelieved by many, from their not being well informed respecting the powers of evaporation.

The communication above alluded to, may probably turn out to be that, between the lakes of Wangara and Fittré; which is described by Edrisi as a part of the track of the salt trade along the the Niger. It may be proper to repeat, that the *Misselád* of the map, answers to the upper part of Edrisi's *Niger*.

ERRATA IN THE GEOGRAPHICAL MEMOIR.

Page 130 line the last, for *whole*, read *given*.
——— 148 — last but one, for *and*, read *to*.
———171, 172 for *Metho*, read *Metko*.

# OBSERVATIONS

## ON THE

# LANGUAGE OF SIWAH

## By WILLIAM MARSDEN, Esq. F. R. S.

*To the Right Honourable Sir* JOSEPH BANKS, *Bart.*

DEAR SIR,

MY curiosity has been much gratified by your obliging communication of Mr. Horneman's specimen of the language spoken at
*Siwah*, or the Oasis of Ammon, in the Lybian Desert; and it will
afford satisfaction to you in return, to be informed, that notwithstanding the accident to his papers, which we must all regret, and
which might cause some doubt to attach to the correctness of a list
subsequently formed, I am enabled to identify the words he has
transmitted, amongst the dialects of Africa with which we are already
acquainted, and thereby to increase the confidence we feel in the
general accuracy of this zealous and enterprising traveller.

Not having any previous knowledge of the extensive people
whom he calls *Tuarick*, of whose language he was given to understand that this of *Siwah* is a dialect, I directed my attention in the
first instance to the numerous specimens I possess of the languages

spoken by various tribes of Negros in the northern part of the continent, but without being able to trace in any of them the slightest
similitude.  I then pursued my comparison through the Arabic, He-
brew, Syriac, Chaldaic, and the different branches of the Ethiopic;
and although I thought some distant affinity perceptible, it was not
such as could be insisted upon.  I was next led to examine the language spoken by the inhabitants of Mount Atlas, known in Morocco
by the names of *Shilha* شلح, and *Breber* or *Berber* بربر, but in
their own country by that of *Amazigh* امازيغ; and here I had the
satisfaction of ascertaining the object of my search.  The following
examples will, I doubt not, be judged sufficient evidence of the language of these countries of *Siwah* and *Shilha*, distant from each
other by the whole breadth of Africa, being one and the same; and
I scarcely need to claim even that reasonable allowance which every
candid person will make for the difference of orthography that unavoidably results from the different circumstances under which
collections of this nature are formed.

|            | Siwah.    | Shilha.               |
|------------|-----------|-----------------------|
| Head,      | *Achfé*,  | *Eghf, Eaghph.*       |
| Eyes,      | *Taun*,   | *Tet, Tetten, Awin*   |
| Hand,      | *Fuss*,   | *Efus, Aphoose.*      |
| Water,     | *Aman*,   | *Aman.*               |
| Sun,       | *Itfuct*, | *Taffought, Tafogt.*  |
| Cow,       | *Ftunest*,| *Tefnast, Taphonest.* |
| Mountain,  | *Iddrarn*,| *Adarar.*             |
| Dates,     | *Tena*,   | *Tini, Teeny.*        |

The earliest account of the *Shilha* language of which I am at
present aware, is that given by Jezreel Jones, in a Latin epistle
published at the end of Chamberlayne's Oratio Dominica, in 1715.
He says, " Lingua Shilhensis vel *Tamazeght*, præter planities *Messæ*,

Hahhæ et provinciam Daræ vel Drâ, in plus viginti viget provinciis regni Sûs in Barbaria Meridionali. Diversæ linguæ hujus dantur dialecti in Barbaria, quæ ante Arabicam, primariam Mauritaniæ Tingitanæ et Cæsariensis provinciarum linguam ibi obtinuêre, et hodiernum inter Atlanticorum Sûs Dara et Reephean Montium incolas solum exercentur." A specimen is added, consisting of about one hundred words. In the excellent account of Morocco published in Danish, by George Höst, in 1779, there is also a short vocabulary of this language, where the words are given with apparent accuracy, in the Arabic character.

Several years ago you were so kind as to transmit for me to Mr. Matra, His Majesty's Consul at Morocco, (a gentleman whose exertions for the advancement of useful knowledge, and particularly of that which is the object of the African Association, deserve the highest praise,) a copy of an extensive alphabetical list of English words, which I printed and distributed with the view of facilitating the attainment of languages not to be met with in dictionaries, and in consequence of which I received from him, through your hands, a very valuable communication. " It is not, (he says in a letter dated in 1791, that accompanied it,) the printed copy Mr. Marsden sent me, but an exact duplicate. His copy, with the words translated into Arabic, is sent to *Tombuctoo*, I fear but with little chance of its returning." That copy never did return; but the transcript I received contains a version of all the words into the Mauritanian dialect of Arabic, for the purpose of enabling a *talb*, or priest, from the *Shilha* country, to write opposite to each, in the same character, the corresponding terms in his language. I have been used to consider this as a very curious document, even when I believed it to apply only to the western coast of Africa, but its importance will be much increased, if we should find, as there is ground to presume, that the *Shilha* or *Berber* extends across the whole continent, in a direction between the Negro dialects on the southern side, and the Moorish or Arabic of the Mediterranean coasts, and that it was the general language of all Northern Africa before the period of the Mahometan conquests. Independently of the Arabic terms, which must ever accompany the progress of that religion, I think it exhibits some strong marks of affinity to that class of Oriental languages which the German writers have distinguished by the name of Shemitic; and if this should be established, (contrary, however, to the opinion of Höst,) it will not be unreasonable to suppose it the ancient Punic, corrupted by the influx of words successively introduced by the colonies or armies of Greeks, Romans, and Goths, and at length mixing again with a branch of the original stream, in its connection with the modern Arabic.

I am, Dear Sir, &c.

W. M.

*Spring Garden, 1st May,* 1800.

P. S. Since writing the foregoing, I have adverted to the chapter on the Oasis of Ammon, in the learned work of my friend Major Rennell, (the Geographical System of Herodotus examined,) and perceive from the extracts he has selected, (p. 589, 590) that Herodotus understood the Ammonians to be composed of Egyptians and Ethiopians, and their language to be formed from a mixture of both, which might have been true in his time; but that the Arabian geographers, Edrisi and Ibn Al Wardi, assert that Santariah (which the Major has proved to be the Oasis of Ammon, or *Siwah*) is inhabited by Berbers mixed with Arabs.

MAY, 1802.

# LIST OF THE SOCIETY,

INSTITUTED 1788, FOR THE PURPOSE OF EXPLORING
THE INTERIOR OF AFRICA.

———————

The Countess of Aylesbury.
The Right Hon. Henry Addington.

The Duke of Buccleugh.
The Marquis of Blandford.
The Right Hon. Sir Joseph Banks,
    Bart. K. B.
The Hon. Thomas Brand.
Richard H. A. Bennet, Esq.
Mark Beaufoy, Esq.
Robert Barclay, Esq.
William Bosville, Esq.
William Burgh, Esq.
Dr. Charles Burney.
N. Boylston, Esq.

The Earl of Carlisle.
The Earl of Carysfort.

Lord Cawdor.
The Hon. Henry Cavendish.
Thomas Coutts, Esq.
Thomas Gray Comings, Esq.

The Marquis of Exeter.
Gerard Noel Edwards, Esq.
The Rev. Francis Egerton.
John Ellis, Esq.
George Ellis, Esq.

Sir Adam Ferguson, Bart.
Colonel Fullarton.

The Duke of Grafton.
Lord Gwydir.
Lord Glenbervie.
The Rt. Hon. Thomas Grenville.

Thomas Gisborne, Esq.
George Gostling, Esq.
Robert Gregory, Esq.

The Earl of Harrington.
The Countess of Harrington.
The Earl of Hardwicke.
Lord Hawke.
Sir Charles Grave Hudson, Bart.
Sir John Hort, Bart.
Charles House, Esq.
Henry Hoare, Esq.
Henry Hugh Hoare, Esq.
Benjamin Hobhouse, Esq.
Everard Home, Esq.

The Earl of Ilchester.
Thomas Johnes, Esq.

R. Payne Knight, Esq.

Lord Louvaine.
The Bishop of Llandaff.
Sir Wilfred Lawson, Bart.

The Earl of Moira.
The Earl of Morton.
Sir Charles Middleton, Bart.
William Marsden, Esq.
Charles Miller, Esq.

James Martin, Esq.
John Maitland, Esq.
Colonel de Meuron.

The Duke of Northumberland.
The Hon. Frederick North.
Sir Richard Neave, Bart.

Lord Viscount Palmerston.
The Hon. John Peachy.
Sir William Pulteney, Bart.
William Morton Pitt, Esq.
Samuel Parker, Esq.

The Duke of Roxburgh.
General Rainsford.
Colonel Roberts.

The Earl of Shaftesbury.
The Earl Spencer.
Sir John Stepney, Bart.
Sir John Sinclair, Bart.
Hugh Scott, Esq.
John Symmons, Esq.
Richard Stonhewer, Esq.
Hans Sloane, Esq.
David Scott, Esq.

The Bishop of Winchester.
Sir Edward Winnington, Bart.

Sir William Watson, Bart.
John Wilkinson, Esq.
Joseph Windham, Esq.
Samuel Pipe Wolfrestan, Esq.
George Wolfe, Esq.
Roger Wilbraham, Esq.

John Willett Willett, Esq.
The Rev. Dr. Winne.

Lord Yarborough.
Sir William Young, Bart.

## HONORARY MEMBER.

Major James Rennell, F. R. S.

## THE COMMITTEE.

The Earl of Moira.
The Bishop of Llandaff.
Right Hon. Sir Joseph Banks, Treasurer.
Sir John Stepney, Bart.
Sir William Young, Bart. Secretary.

*Any Person desirous of becoming a Member of the African Association, is desired to signify the same to a Member of the Committee; or, in Writing, to Mr. Henry Chisholm, Clerk to the Meetings, No. 23, Bridge-street, Westminster.*

N. B. *The Subscription of each Member is Five Guineas annually.*